Reform School!

James E. Billman

This book is non-fiction and fictional.
Real Life adventures are loosely based on
hearsay events and are not intended to depict
any specific individual or location.

Written by James E. Billman
Cover art by Dorothy Robison
Layout by Aztec Printing, Inc.

Copyright 2009 James E. Billman
All rights reserved.

24 Devonshire Drive
Madisonville, KY 42431
270- 821-2848

Cordon Publications

731 C. Erie Ave.
Evansville, Indiana 47715
www.cordonpublications.com
Cora@cordonpublications.com
(812) 303-9070

All reprint rights are reserved except with permission
from the author, James E. Billman, as stipulated under
the U.S. Copyright Act of 1976.

Published by James E. Billman in conjunction with
Cordon Publications

First printing: August 2009.
Printed in the United States of America
ISBN# 978-0-9822083-5-9

Synopsis

Using experience and first-hand knowledge gained from a career in public education, this manuscript presents a critical look at how our schools are failing and includes suggestions for a sweeping national reformation. The chapters examine the various groups that affect the process of education and challenges the paradigms now taken for granted. Thematic throughout is a call for a no-nonsense school environment, nationalization of a curriculum and multiple pathways to graduation that will prepare public school students to function in a global society. The text also includes numerous anecdotes from the author's experiences and five "Real Life Adventure" moral essays.

Dedication

To my wife Karen,

whose patient encouragement,

love and support are always present

to temper my unrest

as well as to lessen my reluctance.

Reform School!

Table of Contents

Prologue

1: Teachers

Real Life Adventure #1

2: Schools

Real Life Adventure #2

3: Students

Real life Adventure #3

4: Parents

Real Life Adventure #4

5: Others

Real Life Adventure #5

6: The Fix

Epilogue

Prologue

Let's start on common ground. 1) We've all been to school and we probably have an opinion about those times, and 2) schools today aren't consistently delivering a quality product. However, there's also uncommon ground that none of us share when speaking of education: no two of us have had 1) the same learning experiences (academic successes and/or failures), and 2) the same recollection of the processes of socialization (call this "fitting in"). So I must actually begin with the task of substantiating myself to you concerning my qualifications in standing on the metaphorical mountain and speaking to others about the direction that education should take. Something must be done; in fact, lots of something must be done. Obviously, I'd like to be that voice.

My opinions might have some credence because I have spent time on both sides of the desk having been involved as a student, a parent and a teacher. I have moved in and out of education three times: 12 school years from 1969 to 1981, 4 ½ school years from 1989 to 1993, and 5 school years between 2001 and 2008. My classroom experience has been in high school science, primarily the physical sciences but also some chemistry, a smattering of biology, and in the vocational programs of a community college teaching math, physics, and optics courses associated with laser technology. I've tutored students and written variously on educational themes.

I moved "in and out" of education because I would get burned out and, in honest self-assessment, feel that my effectiveness was waning primarily for attitudinal as well as sanctimonious reasons. Whatever else, I'd always get bound by the bureaucracy, disgruntled at the misguided leadership of the driving forces of education and my inability to "make a difference" and resign. I would then change directions and get involved in the building trades with no great measure of personal or financial success, which after a few years, would bring me back to teaching with a rekindled passion.

I was never the teacher of the year anywhere, but I can boast of a bevy of highly successful students who cite me as an influential person during their school years. I could certainly be accused and convicted of making my classes challenging by teaching to the higher echelons of students. Retrospectively, I feel that I was patient and understanding on an individual basis, but driven to cover my subject as it might relate to the next higher level. As they say, I saw myself as being "hard but fair." Not that I profess that my methodology in the classroom was the best way, but only that I am qualified to my opinion simply for reasons of having experience and longevity.

Perhaps what I didn't do also qualifies me to voice a learned opinion. I have never been a school administrator, one of the "chosen few" who did all the so-called committee work or a very good team player. (I was too opinionated for the latter two.) Neither could I multi-task nor can I smile on cue. Throughout my career, I could never go into a classroom unprepared and "just let it happen," so I was perpetually disturbed when meetings and "other things" (of which there were many) took time away from classroom preparation. And I was never so naïve to think that I could "talk to the students on their level" back in the days when that was how we educators fooled ourselves as if a classroom full of adolescents had a corporate, singular thought. In all probability most students had then as they do now little to say about education that doesn't have the word "suck" in it.

But I need to be totally honest in my efforts at qualification so I feel a compulsion to list those times when I nearly sold out my convictions of education. During my time at the community college I was a grant coordinator/lead instructor for a program designed to put women and persons of minority into jobs of high technology. At the particular time when the program was announced, it was also a miserable down time for my remodeling and construction business. Under the auspices of a part time job I responded to the posting for a position in the grant for a tutor, but as the result of my interview, the hiring committee thought I would serve well as coordinator/lead instructor of the program. I was honored by their offer and chose to go part time with my business and return to education. It was an eighteen month grant offered as an alternate delivery program (evening and Saturday hours) in which I thoroughly enjoyed and list as the best of times. After the grant was concluded, I applied for and was chosen as a full time instructor in the Advanced Technology Department of the college. While on staff at the college, I enrolled at the University of Iowa seeking a Ph.D. in Management of Community Colleges thinking that I would like to become a department head or a dean in one of the multi-tiered areas of a community college. Had it worked out, had I not become disgruntled with the "good old boy" politics rampant at the college where I worked and had I not been totally turned off by the pomposity of certain professors at the university, I may have become, at least for a little while, what I now profess not to be. (Whew!) Had I not watched the political posturing (butt-kissing) and the "middle-of-the-night" resignation/firing of colleagues who had fallen from grace, I might not be writing this book. There's no doubt some (a lot of?) acrimony in what follows—no excuses.

I also must offer the reason that those in academia will discredit me: I write experientially and not academically. For one who has spent time in education and chooses to write educational treatises, it is important for them to: 1) write formally, 2) to list sources and 3) to cite previous works done by others. I am defying this for the very reason that I am my own source (time and experience) and my assortment of anecdotes, although true, cannot accurately be documented (too much "he said, I said"). Plus who wants to read educational writing that follows a procedure of formality that requires one to base their research from composites of former research? In other words in educational-ese, new ideas are built oh so modestly from previous work that other researchers have done. I respect this process, but I wonder about its workability in the face of today's educational dilemmas; hence, my decision to write from what I have seen and experienced over the course of my career for it seems that the formal method has become a self-consuming beast. For example, what if something based on muddled but accorded research was written and developed with a new twist on an old theme set off all the bells and whistles in the educational department at the State University as being the next great innovation in the field? Say it was even proven in sampling arenas, at the laboratory schools. However, when implemented into the public education arena the great innovative something failed, but went accepted based on the credibility of the institution and the fact that the local school bought the program with big bucks. Educational writing and research has done this in more than a few instances. Perhaps I've overkilled my point and feel the need for contrition in digressing from educational norms. I'm sorry Professors Smith, Jones or Adams, nothing against you as much as against the constraints that bind the process.

So where are the new ideas? Where does change occur? Obviously change has occurred because those involved with schools today realize levels of student achievement are sinking in a quagmire of black ooze that's sucking them forever deeper and deeper into the depths of academic desperation and futility.

Further, one has to understand that education is not a natural science and experiments, even statistically correlated findings, suffer from the dilemma of time and space warp. What happened yesterday may not happen today and what happened over there may not happen here. Or, according to String Theory, what happened here may cause something totally unrelated to happen there. Virtually every teacher agrees that there are years when their classes are smart and years when their classes are not so smart. Much educational research that is cited today is so obsolete that it is ridiculous, but to reduce it to the lowest denominator, the products of education are students who are capable of succeeding not corporately but individually based largely on their experiences in school. As a society, we are firm in our conviction that each of us is different; therefore, my first tenet of change places the power to affect student success in the hands of the teacher who stands at the head of the classroom as an individual and not as an instrument of a process developed on the fifth floor of a college of education hundreds of miles away. Be reasonable, what credibility does that individual on the 5th floor of an educational building at the university who hasn't taught in a high school or, even worse, a junior high school for twenty years actually have? He has no concept of what actual class room management involves because he's not there and won't be there for all the blather and bull crap that comprises so much of a teacher's time because his life as a teacher is occupied with a group of college students who are only too agreeable to acquiesce to the grade they "earn" by being agreeable. Trust that I am disdainful of so much research and have run afoul of certain people of authority throughout my professional career.

    I also write of technology. Textbooks are outdated by the time they reach the classrooms yet they remain in a particular class room on a revolving cycle for as long as seven (ten? even more?) years. Being of the notion that students have to understand the core of a subject before they tackle the ancillaries, I have no great problem with old textbooks. (I do have problems, though, with old textbook full of student-authored anatomical improprieties and injurious references to other people, both teachers and peers.) In rummaging through his books, I discovered that I had students doing the same experiments in physics from textbooks printed in 2004 that my father-in-law did in 1934. It gave me a sense of pride to realize the enduring power of teaching core subjects when I compare the world of '34 with '04.

Another point in suggesting my choice to digress from the norm is to reach out to a typical rather than to an atypical audience. Does that make sense? Do I give a rat's rump if my hypothetical Professors Smith, Jones and Adams that are out of touch with reality in their proverbial ivy covered buildings look disdainfully at a lowly former high school teacher who cops an attitude of necessary change? No. But alas, the professors have the degree and the pontifical clout with peers and with "successful businessmen," (my pet peeve of all time) who somehow feel that because of their position and/or their wealth they are qualified to give their profound advice to administrators and school board members concerning how to teach a classroom full of adolescents. (Notice how teachers weren't mentioned?) Administrators are taught that their job is to teach teachers, and the reason that many administrators became administrators was to escape the classroom in which they weren't very successful. Didn't Einstein himself sometimes appear rather tottering when asked to give his opinion on matters outside his field? ("Tell us Doctor Al, is there a God?")

I also must confess that I did do some research in preparing what I have to say. *No Child Left Behind* (NLCB), for example, was not only an ill-conceived platitude to impress the public but went unchallenged because it sounded good, worked in a few instances in Houston (while failing in many more) and was lofty-sounding. How much money do you suppose has been spent on meeting the expectations and interpretations of *No Child Left Behind*? It did create jobs, albeit useless jobs. The so-called research was credited and the educational agencies grasped the program because not doing so would lead to their not being funded. (Funds that, in reality, never amount to those allocated!) Once again, I lived it and, along with other teachers, knew that the tenets, the very roots of NCLB were unrealistic, hence unattainable. I was there to see what wasn't working, to hear my peers voice the same concerns as me, to smell the stench of failure, to taste the bitterness of defeat as we played the game destined to have no winners and to touch the process ever so slightly because we were trapped inside it. Again, where's my research? I carry it in my heart and transcript it to the following discourse.

I would also ask that you do not misconstrue what a lot of disgruntled teachers claim when they profess to have disliked the substance of teaching but loved to teach (the kids). I cannot put myself in that category either. I did not enjoy looking at vacuous students totally distended from the material being taught who had not given themselves to participation in the learning process. (Mr. Billman, what do I need to know this for?) Yes, there is great satisfaction in the fruits of one's teaching efforts and nothing, absolutely nothing takes the place of a student achieving to succeed for no other reason than for the sake of knowledge, but the aspiring students are dwindling in proportion to those "slackers" who come to school for no other reason than to fulfill the mandates, whether parental or civil. Teachers tell each other to "hang in there" and take their personal repose in the five percent who do want to learn and who do strive to succeed.

I could not do that; hence, my conviction that students should earn the privilege to be in upper level classes—a contention in which I expound upon.

No, I do not profess that the kids are great or that being around and among them keeps a person young. I know that many other teachers say these things and many actually believe it although I strongly suspect that the majority of those teachers who glean great enjoyment, even love, from their students tend to be representative of the earlier grades or teach niche classes that appeal to specific groups of students. However, I don't dispute the validity of these teachers' enjoyment and am happy that so many can take that approach. Generally speaking, I liked the students as individuals and repeatedly told them that I refused to judge a person based on their classroom performance, but rendered grades entirely on classroom performance. My philosophy of education was more a subject-matter approach driven by the material I taught because I believed in the importance of core subjects. Nevertheless, I had a difficult time sitting through umpteen hundred in-services that insisted that we teachers should teach the child first and the subject second. I obviously have felt a need to speak to this in what follows.

Whether I'm qualified or not, this book is something that I feel needs to be said. Is it earth shattering new information and ideas? No. Is it logical, tenable, a priority? Yes, all of the above.

In what follows I offer for your consideration a non-technical commentary about the foibles of education written in vernacular prose. The first part will be discussions and anecdotes of the present state of affairs including such items as the steeped

James E. Billman

bureaucracy, how too many cooks have spoiled the broth, and a lot is written about the apathy that rampantly permeates the entire educational system. The second part obviously has to suggest cures that will not only overhaul how we administer the process but will also offer a proscriptive solution that will put us back on track in delivering meaningful programs of education to deserving, qualified students. I can only hope that my one voice in the crowd will initiate a murmur of discontent that will grow into a public outcry for reform.

1: Teachers

-1-

Each of us has read, heard and seen things with which we disagree. Each of us has formed an opinion or consensus from something that we've read, heard or seen that we did not have previously. And most of us have actually changed our minds from having read, heard or seen something. Others of us kind of waffle through life and tend to be either empathetic or sympathetic to the persuasive side of an issue that is most prominently before us—we're eclectic. I tend to be that way; I gradually formulate an opinion but rarely set it irrevocably in stone.

What follows is my teaching philosophy. It's concise and to the point in stating my belief concerning the role of the teacher and the educational objective in which the teacher operates. I've chosen the words carefully to imply the importance of the work ethic and the understanding that all of us cannot be all things. Yes, we're created equal but we're each individually gifted and handicapped. The role of education is to offer opportunity, the role of the teacher is to facilitate the opportunity for the student, and the role of the student is to take advantage of those

James E. Billman

opportunities provided.

Statement of Teaching Philosophy

I feel that education should be an available, ongoing opportunity transcending barriers of disability, race, gender and age; therefore, making the challenge to learn skills and/or gain knowledge for personal fulfillment a right for each of us. The door to the educational process should always be accessible, which does not mean that the treasures within are granted; they must be earned.

Instructors at all levels of education must understand that their job goes beyond the classroom and success in teaching is measured in student achievement far into the future and not only in the present term. Teachers must recognize learning styles as well as student needs and make their classes relevant to time, space and community. Good education begins and ends with communication. Teachers should strive to be friendly, but not to be a friend; to be challenging, but to also be reasonable; and to keep score, but not to judge.

Students must be conditioned by the teachers to accept challenge, to struggle at times with frustration and to expect difficulty in understanding new concepts and techniques. Students, particularly in higher grades, should be brought to understand time management, to prioritize goals and to value critical and retrospective thinking.

The Army's *Methods of Instruction* course summarized it pretty well for me over forty years ago when the instructor told us how to make a classroom presentation when he said, "Tell them what you're going to tell them, tell them, and then tell them what you told them." To this I would add "Be sure to show them how to do it and finally have them show you that they did it."

-2-

We all have had teachers in our lives. We also know that, just for the sake of classification, there are formal and informal learning situations and which is which depends mostly on the setting—where the learning took place. Schools are traditionally thought to be institutions of learning in a formal setting whereas Mom showing her child how to make a cheese omelet is likely to be seen as a setting of informal learning. I disagree with this notion and feel that a better discernment might come from the manner in which the learning takes place. If the teaching and subsequent learning came as the result of a plan, it's formal, and all the other stuff associated with the formal objective is informal. To my way of thinking, Mom teaching her child how to prepare a cheese omelet is just as formal as a high school student learning how to do a mass-mass calculation in chemistry. An informal example, among many other things, would be derived from the dignity, professionalism and conscientiousness perceived by the learner whether making an omelet at home or doing chemistry calculations at school.

Briefly recall a favorite teacher. When I do this, my recollection allows me to remember more about him as a result of the way he was (the informal lesson) than the subject matter he taught formally. Because I was impressed with this teacher's mannerisms and methodology and because his persona captured my attention, so did the formal lesson that he was presenting. He was focused on the subject, professional in his decorum and even instilled a little fear in me, and contrary to my track record in previous classes, I found myself earning an "A" grade. My favorite teacher was my dad. It's imaginable that the converse can also be true if a teacher does not project a positive informal aura. The first impression, which is totally informal, sets the stage for all that follows. Informal learning is ongoing but also fickle; what may have been positive yesterday isn't necessarily that way today. Woe unto those teachers that feel a need to modify their informal character by trying to be like their students—it's a big-time mistake unless that type of teacher wants a short career in teaching as well as risking exposure as a phony. The driving axioms go like this: 1) Be friendly but don't be a friend, and 2) in order to get respect you have to give respect.

Informal learning paves the way for formal learning. In going back to the omelet example, because of her lofty position in her child's mind Mom has the earned respect of her child and the formal lesson flows smoothly as long as previously nurtured ingredients are present such as patience, understanding and knowing that a child's hands aren't as dexterous as an adult's. Each subsequent time that Mom and child begin with a positive informal learning relationship (it's a two-way street) the interpersonal bond between parent and child is strengthened and sets the tone for formal learning. As long as the relationship of informal learning remains and is consistent, the formal learning goes much smoother. When changes occur in the informal perception, the formal learning is affected either for the better or for the worse. In other words, if the learners have not made themselves "learnable" informally, there won't be much happening formally.

Make no mistake, if the teacher has impressed the student informally in a manner that puts the student in a frame of mind conducive to formal learning, that's good. However, informal learning obviously can be affected other ways when considering all the miscellaneous other stimuli that come into focus on a daily basis. Even though a student may come into class with all the best intentions, there may be informal deterrents initiated by events of the day, something that has been disturbing in the home life, a disruptive classmate—any of a number of things. Seldom would any of these be conducive to improving the informal setting and they can be multiplied by 27 if that is the number of students in the class.

I don't want to appear too glib with this formal-informal relationship because it's like most qualitative measurements, there's no clear line of demarcation and it's pretty evident there is a good atmosphere for learning when there's harmony between learner and teacher. Rapport as a result of informal learning also speaks well for fewer of those "down" days where the student lacks focus for so many reasons. But it's also pretty evident that it isn't going to be harmonious with all 27 of the hypothetical students in the classroom at any given time, and that effective teaching of all 27 isn't going to happen at any time no matter how good the teacher is. This is a major, major problem with schools today and the first of many times that I will point to the notion that school should be a privilege for a student and not a right.

There are students who can learn formally in spite of informal perceptions and often they do exactly that because they have the ability to prioritize objectives. The characteristic ability that good students exhibit in being able to say "I'm motivated to learn in spite of the instructor" is truly an admirable trait whether inherited, ingrained at home or acquired through maturity. A reasonable adult person would think that a young student would be rather silly to do something other than put forth his best effort, but students often don't fit that mold. The adage that "you can't use logic on a child and you can't reason with a teenager" is rather applicable and raises the question of whether a specific student should be in a class for no other reason than "just because."

Before leaving this thought of formal and informal learning it is worth mentioning that much informal learning takes place subconsciously too. People are not so much self-analyzers of every action and reaction that they have. I've said things like, "for some reason I just couldn't get much from that class" without seeking to determine what that reason was when I probably could have found it with a little introspection. Other comments such as "I couldn't hear the teacher," and "he didn't speak clearly" are pretty common, but often come too late to do much about them. Again it is pretentious to think that a teacher with 27 students in front of her is going to positively impress everyone in the room with her lovely and winning persona, but the teachers that made their mark on us had something about them that triggered us informally in such a manner that made us receptive to the formalities of the subject.

-3-

What is learning? I've heard two rather interesting hypotheses. The more common notion is that learning comes as a result of sensorial information being absorbed and consequently stored for later use. When we recall something, we reach back into the web of neurons and run it backward. Now the more that particular something is used, the easier it becomes to recall it, kind of like a trail through a forest. The more the trail is traveled the easier it is to follow. There's been a lot said recently about this as brain research is one of the newer frontiers of medical research.

The second hypothesis is rather abstract and speaks to the fact that the molecules that comprise each of us have been around for a long time before they came to be a specific part of us, and they will remain for a long time after they leave us; in fact, forever. When these molecules that have endured time and space come together to form a human being, they act cooperatively and thusly ingrain us with the knowledge of their experiences and travels through history. Since molecules are rather unpredictable things, they come and go but those billions and billions remaining still retain the knowledge of the ages for they are no less or no more than the molecules that left to go somewhere else. This hypothesis suggests that learning is a process of triggering stored molecular information that is held compositely to release itself; hence, learning is more a process of awakening by suggestion what is already there.

Diametrically opposed to each other, one hypothesis says that learning is a process of impaction and the other says that learning is a process of extraction. I actually find more credence in the latter than in the former primarily because the second hypothesis allows for critical thought, the rather unique process that allows us to fashion new ideas from what we know. For example, we know "A" as fact, we know B" as a fact, and we can assimilate something that we didn't formerly know, "C" as a fact. Perhaps I see no cookies in the jar and I knew that there was one cookie left in the jar a while ago, and I notice cookie crumbs on Johnny's lips and his shirt. I'll leave the critical aspect to you.

Either way we might perceive the learning experience, it is a specific process that has three components: there must be 1) a transmitter, 2) a receiver and 3) a medium. Understanding learning this way defines it as nothing beyond merely communicating.

So yes, learning is communication. The transmitter is the sender of the communication, the receiver is the recipient and the medium is the link that connects the first two. Put another way, the teacher is the transmitter, the student is the receiver and the subject material is the medium that links the two together. If any of the components are missing there is no learning. If the teacher is transmitting a medium of information and there is no receiver, there is no learning. If there is no material, there is no communication and the same can be said if there is no transmitter. A textbook is a transmitter with a medium, but not a receiver. Concomitant, or instantaneous learning, can also identify with the three components. This is similar to the classic question whether or not a tree that falls in a forest makes a noise if there is no one to hear it. According to the definition, for sound to exist there must be a falling tree, a medium to carry the vibrations of sound and an ear to hear it.

A nuance to this explanation of learning that really makes it successful is that, when face-to-face, the transmitter must also be capable of receiving and the receiver must be capable of transmitting because true communication is a two-way process. Learning is also an exchange of information. Perhaps oversimplified in my explanation, the process is nevertheless simple: If the receiver can't transmit or the transmitter can't receive, there is no learning. This is the prime culprit in education's failure—the reception isn't very good with 27 students in the classroom because there's too much distorting static.

-4-

What then is the nature of a teacher? It's been said that we are all teachers but in developing a representative example of a teacher based on all the professional educators in the United States, one would get a rather typical graphic describing an average American citizen that wouldn't tell us very much. As some students would argue to the contrary, teachers *are* human with all the sensory receptors and organs that other humans have, which means yes, they have a heart. As difficult as it is in representing any group of large numbers, no teacher can speak for all teachers. There would be a few qualifiers that would present a somewhat skewed demographic: public school teachers have a college degree, they have a license to teach a particular group of students based on the assumption that they have been taught how to teach, they have moderate subject-area expertise and they have an introductory understanding of psychology—these types of things. Beyond this, teachers are nothing uncommon or out of the ordinary.

It doesn't take much imagination to think that a majority of teachers were fairly successful as students and most of them look back on their school experiences as being generally pleasant. Some, of course, chose to teach in an effort to correct the wrongs they experienced, but as stated previously, many teachers can usually name one or two of their teachers who had a major influence on them. All in all, one could say that a teacher is a cut from the mold of other teachers, yet deviations from the norm exist among the teacher group just as with the general population.

A couple of clichés come to mind in describing teachers as a composite. Most of us have heard "if you can't do, teach" and "teachers teach as they were taught." There's truth as well as exceptions to both. A professor I had, when speaking extraneously, was fond of saying, "…That's generally true, but like all generalities they are generally false." For example, consider this statement: "Generally speaking, smart parents have smart kids," which is generally true however you look at the statement. As we know, a person can get into a mess using generalities to describe groups of people whether they be from the general (I tried to resist using the word, but just couldn't.) public or a specific demographic group.

I feel that this brings a necessary discussion of statistics into light, but let me keep it brief. Statistically speaking, something needs to be correlated if it is to be accurately depicted or described, which means that this hypothetical something being tested has to be supported by numbers that are often expressed in percents. Because of the way the postulate is stated (it must be positive), statistical correlation requires 98% agreement. Case in point: we know smart parents have smart kids; because we see it day after day. This concept is not statistically correlated because it doesn't happen 98% of the time, not even close. Smart parents *generally* have smart kids yet our generality can still be meaningful but is without the support of statistics. However, in the world of educational appropriations it is pretty difficult to get funding without supporting statistics; a subject that itself opens a new can of worms when the statistics are skewed or inconclusive.

The point of the discussion about statistics is this: National, state and even local indicators rarely correlate within a teacher's own, specific classroom. No matter what the statistics say, a teacher lives, breathes, eats and sometimes can't help but sleep in his or her own little biosphere occupied by those 27 students, which is why the teacher has had all that coursework that qualifies them to teach. I would humbly suggest that in making statistics and methodology available to a teacher that they would still be given the autonomy to lead his or her classroom in the manner he or she chooses. It's the teacher who knows the "personality" and creates a classroom culture by listening to the heartbeat of a particular group of students. And one more thing in passing, a teacher looks at things from a different point of view and undoubtedly observes that *smart kids tend to have smart parents.*

We also hear that statistics can be interpreted to say whatever a person wants them to say, which isn't true for a well-done case study. The point here is that in education it's very, very hard to produce a good statistic because of all the variables. For example the item being tested has to be accurately stated and precisely measured for validity. The word *accurate* refers to the ability of the person to take the necessary measurements, and the word *precise* refers to the instruments used in making the measurements. Suffice it to say that statistics are potent devices when used correctly as we see in examples of political polls in the newspapers, and they're misconstrued when not used properly. Another statistically meaningful word is *validity*, which teachers often question when they hear an "expert" in education begin a presentation with "Statistics show…" That's when the eyes roll right before they close as the audience settles in for a midday nap.

Suffice it to say, that describing groups of people in terms of statistics often leads to confusion and a whole bunch of other things, particularly if the statistics are not thorough. We see in the news and hear people talking about such things as false positives, true negatives, etc. Teachers take classes in statistics and perhaps this is why they, as a group, become rather disdainful of "new" research that comes down the pike way more often than they are likely to accept it.

Not only in the case of statistics, but teachers also develop a healthy skepticism about many other aspects to which they are exposed. If you'd like to see expressions of bad attitude and feel the aura of bad vibrations so strongly that they can form rain clouds, (try to) teach a group of teachers at an in-service. It is my personal conviction that in-service meetings first came about because administrators thought teachers had too much free time so "by God, we'll give them something to do."

The Law of Entropy, often presented in conjunction with the 2nd Law of Thermodynamics, essentially says that the universe is moving toward chaos. Sometimes the word "chaos" is replaced with the word "disorder" and the Law of Entropy is employed to mean that the universe is moving from being ordered to becoming disordered. There are indeed a lot of examples that bear this out that range from the event of the big bang to the sublimating moth balls in Aunt Bertha's closet, but even if we are moving in that direction, it is not to say that we can't affect much of it. An example of this might be my workspace. Sure, after a week's use it gets pretty messy (disorganized), but I can fix this. Another example could be that a writer's thoughts tend to get pretty random so they have to be organized. (Notice this writer's use of numbers to categorize, list and stay organized as he struggles to offset the Law.) There are indeed many pockets of organization in the universe and in a rather appropriate manner, the Law of Entropy might define a teacher as one who brings order to students; however, as a group these teachers are very chaotic, very disordered and do tend to head off in a variety of tangents. As with the previously mentioned String Theory, The Law of Entropy can certainly be extended to expose some problems in school and classroom management.

In describing teachers it's safe to say that they are pretty dedicated; albeit more dedicated to their subject (content) and to their subjects (students) than they are to authority, mandates and rules that govern them. There's a dichotomy in this because teachers certainly give their students a list of classroom rules that are above and beyond normal school rules, but teachers themselves are rather resentful of being driven by rules. It is obviously confounding when students are expected to know and adhere to several sets of rules that are at least a little different for each teacher because teachers get rather set in their ways.

Are we missing something here—something that speaks to the presence of a double standard? (Remember Pink Floyd's

James E. Billman

lyrics, "Teacher, leave those kids alone.") If the list of school rules would set the tempo of decorum for all classrooms, it might be easier for students to adhere to them. If teachers are disdainful of willy-nilly rules and mandates, one would also think that students would be too. Teachers are at fault and should understand that students would perform better if held to a single, inclusive, realistic set of rules handed down by the administration. Once given these rules, the teachers need to get together and everyone do their part to provide the consistency necessary for a smoothly operating school. In many cases the teachers who enforce the rules are held in contempt by the students because of the teachers who let rules slide. It's easier for these teachers to look the other way than to step up with a unified effort.

Ask a science teacher who teaches a laboratory course to have his or her students now begin to write their lab reports using one of the four different learning styles in which he or she is most comfortable (interpersonal, understanding, mastery and self-expressive). There's immediate skepticism because for years the science teacher has had students write reports using Detective Joe Friday's method from the old television show "Dragnet." In every show, Joe would say "Just the facts, Ma'am." It is pretty difficult for the science teacher to find the merit of a lab report when a student starts to expound on his or her "feelings" about the boiling point of water. Comments like "I think water will not boil until you aren't looking," and "Water boils at 212 degrees because God made it that way," or "Here teacher, I drew a picture of the water boiling." If you want to watch blood boil, watch a science teacher being told to have his students write laboratory

Reform School

reports according to their learning style.

I digress; why would a science teacher be told to have his students write in a variety of ways? Imagine a scenario where an educational specialist at a level worthy of his lofty title(s) notices that students having been deemed worthy of becoming high school graduates can't write very well. The impetus for this observation may have come by looking at test scores in English and completing some well-intended research that included writing samples. Next, the snowball rolls down hill gathering momentum and more research is done until the conclusion is formed: "Students must be able to demonstrate that they can form sentences and express ideas in writing." And the chorus of administrators and educational puppets agrees resoundingly with their refrain, "Damn right they should." So now every non-teacher in the free world of public education and beyond agrees to the following prescription: "All teachers will require their students to write meaningful declarative, interrogative, expositional and exclamatory sentences." Boom, the bomb has dropped. The word "Teachers" from the mandate is unmistakably clear and means all teachers in all areas—science teachers, band teachers, physical education teachers and yes, the English teachers.

It's true that students can't write very well; students don't do a lot of things very well, and to a large degree teachers must shoulder their share of the blame. Probably half of graduating seniors from America's high schools can't explain the seasons, put Jesus, Aristotle and Genghis Kahn in chronological order or factor the number 36. Should lack of scientific, historical and mathematical knowledge call for all teachers requiring their students to show proficiency in science, history and mathematics?

James E. Billman

Obviously not, but possibly so; I will argue this later. But for now one can see the futility of mandates such as "Teachers will require..." and how it sends horrific vibrations throughout the teaching domain.

    Absolutely, teachers of English in my example could have averted this entire issue by making certain that a student with a passing grade could indeed write each of the four types of sentences as well as put their ideas into writing. So why didn't they make their students do these things? Reasons are as diverse as teachers themselves. Would you like to read themes of 27 students in your classes that meet five times each school day in the time you have? Can you even read their scribbled writing that some other teacher didn't teach them how to do? Do you have time to read them when you have hall duty, morning duty, faculty meetings, ticket duty for tonight's game, and even a family, a grocery list and other obligations? Would you like that same disruptive jerk back in your class again next term? The plea goes out that the English teachers need help so rather than proscriptively decrease the load on the teacher and then hold them to reasonable expectations, the gurus of education decide to involve all the teachers in making Johnny a better writer because A) we're all responsible professionals; B) other teachers don't have as great a workload; C) it's mandated so you will do it; D) all of the above.

    Even though it's masked somewhat thinly, teachers are just as eager as students for the end of the day, for Fridays, for holidays and for vacations. I'd like a dollar for every time I heard a teacher refer to the time left before a break signaling the end of something—the period, the day, lunch, you name it. There should be a picture in the National Archives of a teacher pointing to the heavens as they leave school on Friday. I have heard only a single teacher comment "I live for this!" upon entering school on Monday, but I sure heard it when they left on Friday. "Hang in there" is the motto of the teacher. Wouldn't the knowledge that the people at school really don't want to be there suggest that something needs to be done?

Another demographic that typifies and separates a teacher from the mainstream is the attrition rate. Needless to expound on it, but the investment necessarily made to become a teacher is rather expensive, particularly in view of the return on the investment. Several universities now require a Master's Degree for licensure and most recommend it. There are a lot of hoops to jump through on the way to getting the statement of competence that all teachers need to enter a classroom. And there are a lot, lot more today than there were forty years ago. I know of several individuals who completed the three and a half years of course work to become a teacher only to get scared away or weeded out during their time as a student teacher, and I have often heard that the first years are the most critical. "They" say that as high as forty percent of teachers have left the field before they've spent five years in the class room.

I get "warped" in the space-time thing quite frequently, but it's definitely true that the "Times, they are a'changin.'" (Okay, no more song references this chapter.) When I began teaching, corporal punishment in Iowa was okay and was even encouraged. A fellow teacher once came into a bathroom where I was confronting a student for some infraction or another and quite encouragingly told me to "Smack him!" I didn't, but I did put a throat hold on his brother for squirting water on another student during science lab. During these times, I watched a principal whack a student with a fraternity paddle so hard that the student made such a desperate gasp sucking in air that I thought he was going to swallow his tongue.

Yeah, corporal punishment was a bad rule because it wasn't fair for two reasons. The sixty year old English teacher down the hall couldn't issue it with as much force as me, and it sent the message to students that if you hit me, I'm going to hit you back. To continue my incident with the kid who was the recipient of the choke hold, he was first pulled away from his lab station to be verbally reprimanded, and his reaction was to take a swing at me which resulted in my reaction. Times were indeed different and pendulums do swing...

And different grew on different. School shootings and student reprisals still make big news and I would dare say they will become more and more common if we continue on the present course. At the community college where I taught I observed a teacher's tires that were slashed during the day by an angry student who was easily identifiable by the teacher due to a confrontation she had had earlier. ("Nothing we can do except report it," the department head told her). I didn't even bother to report the student who, when given a zero on a test for blatant copying, showed me his knife just to remind me that he always had it with him. ("You see this here knife I gots?") I knew that because he hadn't personally threatened me there'd be "nothing we can do," plus I would be asked what I had done to provoke the student to this point. Stuff like, "Have you seated him too closely to another student so it is easy for him to cheat? Could you be placing too much pressure on the poor chap? Well, haven't we all cheated at one time or another?"

Having started teaching long ago when corporal punishment was sanctioned, I have had trouble remembering to keep my hands off students (the "don't touch" rule followed the ban of corporal punishment) as I'd gently "help" them adhere to the rules and get through the day with no other problems.

In the small school where I taught for most of my career I usually knew the combatants when fights broke out and also usually knew that both of them probably had no business being called a student in the first place so I'd get to the fracas and break it up just after a few blows had been struck. It was the case in many student fights, to find that one or both of the would-be fighters hoped that a teacher would get to the scene and break it up before it went any further. Old timers like me tell the story how the school used to have boxing gloves and those who wanted to fight got the opportunity to do so in gym class. The new era, on the other hand, experiences girls fighting girls, boys fighting boys as well as more than a couple instances of girls fighting boys.

The 1955 movie *Blackboard Jungle* shows a scene where Glenn Ford and a colleague unsuccessfully punch it out with a group of students that includes Sidney Poitier. The Gangs known as the Crips and Bloods from the '70's both originated largely as high school groups became "organized." I expound further on this issue later, but rare is the school where one or more teachers aren't struck or attacked on an annual basis. Is it television with all the "reality" shows, dysfunctional families and violence? Society, ethnicity, morality—what then? How about the *critical mass* hypothesis as an explanation from a science teacher? When things (the 57 varieties of subatomic particles) get packed together too tightly in the nucleus of an atom, the binding energies aren't sufficient to hold the nucleus together and the larger atom splits into simpler atoms amidst the release of energy. Perhaps our school populations are too large and students are packed too tightly.

One might think that athletic teams and school activities are a release stimulus and because of these offerings schools should be peaceful places of co-existence. Put the numbers to it. In a school of 1200 students of which 600 are boys, there is one boy's varsity basketball team where 12-15 students dress for the games and usually not more than seven of them plays. Basketball lasts four months, the school year for more than nine. Yes there's more than one team, but you see the point. Schools are violent places the way they are structured and it is getting worse.

That teachers aren't paid very well is a typical remorse from within the ranks. As previously alluded, comparing national averages of those with equivalent levels of education to teacher salaries lies as the cause for such concern. Teachers are, for the most part, public employees and those teachers in private schools usually have their salaries set a little lower than the public schools so it's no secret what a teacher earns. Teachers pretty well know what they are getting into when making a career choice to teach; it's a conscious, premeditated choice where few if any prospective educators enter the field to make money and get rich, but also one where none of them starve from lack of funds to buy food.

Reform School

  Many teacher salary schedules are comprised of a grid based on two things, time spent teaching and the educational level of the instructor, which allows for the teacher to progress horizontally (professional educational attainment) as well as vertically (years of service). For example, if the base rate for a beginning teacher is $28,000/year, this is what a beginning teacher with a bachelor's degree would earn. If the increments at this school were based on four percent both horizontally and vertically, a teacher with a master's degree in education and six years experience would have moved three spaces horizontally (B.A. plus 15 hours, B.A. plus 30 hours, master's) and six spaces vertically, one for each year. This puts the teacher at $28,000 + (28,000 x .04 x 3) + (28,000 x .04 x 6) = $38,080/year, which is still not very good compared equivalently to several other professional occupations. There is also extra pay for other things and there are a lot of other things in a school like football, concert band, theater, cross-country, and other organization too numerous to list. So a 6-year experienced head football coach paid at 12% of his current contract of $38,080 now earns another $4570/year (38,080 x .12 = $4570) bringing his salary to $42,650. A teacher also gets this incremental raise fairly automatically just by signing a contract for the next year and not so much by having exhibited competency. Literally, perseverance pays off because with no effort on the part of the teacher, the teacher's union representatives negotiate annually for him with the school board for a raise based on the base contract. All teachers are lumped together with no case made for competency or merit. For purposes of calculation, imagine the negotiators fought tooth and nail for a base of 28,500/year, up from the previous $28,000 and won. They got a whopping 1.78% raise, but our football coach now gets an annual salary of $28,500 + (28500 x .04 x 3) + (28500 x .04 x 7) = $39,900 + (39900 x 0.12) = $44,688 and it really becomes a 4.56 % raise, which isn't too awfully bad in circles of comparison, especially if the coach did not have to say anything to anyone about getting a raise and his team went 2-9. There are obviously different schedules throughout the country, but this is a typical one, and football may have not been such a good example of extra income considering that some high school football coaches earn in excess of six figures. Actually, salary schedules do show that a teacher with twenty years service really isn't so bad comparatively as he or she progresses regardless of performance and with the understanding that teaching in the same field at the same school most likely gets easier as time passes. No wonder that it has been said that teaching rewards mediocrity because it is easy to fall into a rut and do the same thing year after year. In some cases, one could say that obsolescence pays. This grid method is undergoing scrutiny and gradually changing to reward competency with programs such as the National Merit Teacher certification and similar programs. Many teachers don't like the thought of changing from this older version and why would they?

So…why teach. Frankly, I don't know. There must be a pretty long list of individual "why's" including a love of kids, wanting to make a difference, sharing experiences, feeling that one has something special to offer and just the plain old notion that "it'd be neat to be a teacher." After a period of time, teachers find other reasons than money to persevere such as the summer vacations, seasonal breaks, habit (once established, it does get

Reform School

easier from one year to another—up to a point), not knowing what else they'd do, and retirement benefits. Single reasons do not often answer complex questions; I imagine that most long-term teachers can honestly answer that they have found a measure of successfulness in their profession. No doubt that a good many teachers like what they do even though they may not enjoy the moment, but when considering everything, the long-term "goods" outweigh the thousands of momentary "bads." Aren't most jobs and even life itself that way? It may have been a horrible fourth period, but a single insightful comment by a student in sixth period can make a teacher's day. One thing is true for "lifers," the teacher gets a year older each year, but his or her students remain the same age. However as the age disparity increases between student and teacher, the time to retirement gets closer and closer.

    Teachers therefore, are a comparison of contrasts. There are good teachers and poor teachers; there are dedicated teachers and teachers who are there only to collect a paycheck; and there are probably some teachers with six fingers on one hand. Life streams by with all sorts and kinds. As a group, teachers are generally (!) a bunch of good people whose classrooms have been overly infiltrated by outside forces that put more pressure on them than is fair. Outcomes-based measurements assess teacher effectiveness in so many places and every teacher has a principal who has erroneously been given the job of assessing them. But one thing remains, you can't make chicken salad out of chicken poop.

James E. Billman

Real Life Adventure #1

Springtime, when love springs eternal is the time when teachers are asked to be particularly wary of students breaching the school's Discipline Code that addresses personal displays of affection, often referred to as PDA. On the rare occasion that a teacher notices two students rubbing against each other and/or kissing in the hallway, he or she is contract bound to "remind" the offenders of the code disallowing such activity. Sometimes the teacher merely says "PDA" to them and continues on his or her merry way knowing that the students will immediately come to their senses and return to the proper frame of mind. "These nasty hormones," the two offending students declare embarrassingly to each other, "we need to work on suppressing them." Not so in reality.

The teacher who says "PDA" and doesn't stop whatever she's doing isn't doing her job according to a clause in the contract that nebulously refers to "other duties as assigned," which obviously includes enforcement of rules. Going from the sublime to the ridiculous, does this mean the teacher is supposed to stand there to make sure that the students heed her demand and follow the rules? Should she chastise them with a

Reform School

stern lecture concerning amoral behavior and the respect (and anguish) that abstinence brings? Should she give the offenders a detention? She probably doesn't even know their names and the students probably would tell her their names were something like Anthony and Cleopatra. Should she send them to the principal's office? That action however, requires a note explaining the situation and for the note to be signed by the teacher which will make her even later to her class—as if she even had the proper referral form with her. Should she personally take the students to the principal's office and explain to him that these students were violating the school's sacrosanct rules and regulations concerning personal displays of affection? The principal would raise a reprehending eyebrow at her for leaving her classroom full of students who by now are approaching critical mass. Or should she take the offenders with her to her classroom, get the form, write them up and then send them to the principal or to the D-hall (detention room), but that will make class start late and she knows her students will be wasting valuable class time while she fills out the form.

    What to do? When she was in college, a professor in a methods course told the class to "pick your battles wisely. Let some little things go but stick to your guns on the big issues." So the teacher resolves the issue by taking out her Glock semi-automatic pistol and fires at Will and Wilma thereby resolving her dilemma. "Ha! That'll teach them."

    In reality, the teacher breaks stride, looks at the offenders and tells them to break it up, which has the effect of a belch in a tornado, and keeps going to her class. There's no way for teachers to stop these kinds of clear student violations and still get the job done in the classroom. Let the principal figure out a way to enforce these rules. Perhaps she will ask him how a teacher can enforce all the rules at the next faculty meeting. Administratively trained principals respond to questions of this nature with statements such as, "Students are more likely to behave and follow the rules if they know a teacher is present," as he mentally put the questioning teacher on his S-list.

A lot of teachers feel that such an occasion as this would be a good time for a rule change allowing the discretionary use of the fire hose since a jab to the kidneys or a bamboo shoot to the back of the thighs is classified as corporal punishment. Or, how about segregation as studies (who, when, where?) seem to support that same sex schools and/or classes work pretty well where they've been tried, although it's not feasible in smaller districts.

Yes, it would be nice to think that breaking up near-copulative embraces are met with an amicable, quick response and statements of chagrined regret as the two mortified students hurry away to class so they can have their textbooks and notebooks open by the time the bell rings. But it doesn't happen. It's usually a surly grunt by the boy and a look of utter hatred by the girl.

Teachers find themselves in some embarrassing situations over dress codes too. There's a generation gap many of us simply don't understand because it defies all sense of reasonability why a girl wants her boobs to hang out and why a boy wants the belt line of his pants to be so low he has to walk around holding them up. I'm sure if "studies" were made comparing high school students who, according to a notion of reasonability to us old folks, dress themselves within reason vs. students who dress unreasonably results would overwhelmingly show some "revealing" conclusions. Modestly dressed students are more popular and do better in school than students who conspicuously attempt to "lower" the dress code.

But there has to be a PDA rule and a dress code because, well just because. In my freshman biology class of 17 girls, none of which were over fifteen, three of them were mothers.

Another school situation that occurs in the springtime is that nerves are frazzled, the end of the year is in sight and everyone is tired of the same old grind. It's not uncommon to see tempers flair and confrontations result, and it is not always between students. Students who have not done much in class want extra credit so they can bring their grade up. Parents e-mail teachers wondering whether there might be a "personality" conflict between the teacher and their beloved child; in other words, it is the teacher's fault for their child's poor performance. Teachers are just fed up with all the distractions outside the classroom and all the inattention inside the classroom. It's a tough time for all.

Once upon a time there was a teacher in the spring of the year who removed an unruly student from class. The teacher had stopped her lesson three times on account of the same student, and had asked her to please be still and to kindly quit being a distraction to the rest of the class to which the student replied, "I ain't bein' no distraction. You the distraction. No one's listenin' to you no how."

The teacher walked toward the student, stood by her but not facing her and told her in her most stern voice to leave class and report to the principal's office. "That's bull shit" the student recounted as she slammed her book on her desk, picked up her notebook, knocked over her chair when she stood up, threw her notebook in the waste can and stomped out the door amid profanity-laced personal innuendos toward the teacher.

As the student continued her tirade while going down the hallway, the teacher moved to the doorway of the classroom and stood watching. Another teacher poked his head out and made the "shh" sound as the student passed his open doorway and then returned to his lesson. The student, perhaps sensing that the teacher who had removed her from class was watching, stopped, turned around, came back and said that she wanted her notebook that she had thrown in the waste can. The teacher remained steadfast in the doorway blocking the student's return and was taken by surprise when the student began to scream and to pummel her with her fists.

Having been totally surprised when hit, the 110 pound, 40+ year old teacher was temporarily stunned and in no condition to defend herself against the out-of-control student who continued to pound on her teacher, and when she fell to the floor, the student commenced kicking her. A student in the class finally had the preservation of mind to get out of his seat and pull the attacking student away from the teacher. As he held firmly onto the student, an assistant principal who had been alerted by the second teacher arrived. The principal promptly called for the school's Resource Officer (a deputy sheriff) who came, subdued the girl, took her out of the room, handcuffed her and called dispatch for someone to take her to jail.

It shouldn't have to be mentioned, but unfortunately

tensions still exist in America and its high schools, so imagine that the student was African-American, the teacher, the alerting teacher, the intervening student, the assistant principal, and the resource officer were Caucasian. Or turn it around if the story reads better.

    As a precautionary measure, a perhaps too quick-thinking school official called the state highway patrol and by the time they arrived in force (three cars) it was during "passing time." When the student body saw the troopers and sheriff's deputies in the building between classes, the rumors instantaneously flew as a potentially volatile situation developed. Let's say that in this case nothing escalated beyond some racial posturing, promises of reprisal from both sides of the issue, and later, some pretty nasty phone calls and e-mails sent to some school officials. All said, the administration did a nice job of de-fusing it.

    The teacher was taken to the hospital by another school employee so no ambulance was involved to further fuel the speculative fire. She was treated for cuts and abrasions and released; she had no broken bones but did incur a sprained wrist when she fell to the floor. She did not return to the classroom for the rest of the year. The student, a junior, was booked for assault and spent 25 days in a juvenile detention center.

    Long after the physical pain was gone, the emotional anguish remained for both the teacher and the student.

    As in every account of this nature, there could be a lot more added to the story such as community history, past confrontations, mindsets of both the teacher and student toward each other, location of the school in the United States, and all the "I said-you said" stuff that emerges in the aftermath of confrontation. And even the two people involved couldn't list the innumerable intangibles that festered and boiled prior to the student attacking the teacher. It is very unlikely to assume there was only this single provocation for the student, whether real or imagined. Fill in the blanks yourself, but whatever the case, this was *the* event of the year for this school; it was bigger than any of the sports rivalries, bigger than prom, and far, far bigger than standardized tests. I refer to it as an event because there is nothing, absolutely nothing that takes precedence over a fight in a school. The very mention of the word evokes about the same reaction, but in the opposite direction, as someone shouting "fire" in a theater.

The next day a faculty meeting was hastily called under the thinly-veiled guise of explaining the situation so the teachers would understand exactly what happened. Actually the newspaper gave a better account. The real intent of the meeting was to "suggest" that teachers not talk about the altercation to other people in the community because of possible legal ramifications. Everyone knows it as the "gag" rule and it is invoked in varying degrees throughout different schools depending mostly on the relationship at the time between the school and the community.

A few weeks later, the school year ended but there was still an issue—what, if any disciplinary measures would be taken to demonstrate parity and equity to those individuals involved? If the student was to be expelled, a volatile racial situation could arise; if she were to be reinstated and allowed back in school, the teachers could rebel citing a lack of leadership. In the final analysis it was the school board's decision, for they were the elected officials who represented the best interests of their constituency in school matters. After all, that is *their* job.

Allow a quick digression for me to say that being on the school board is a thankless job for the most part so a person almost has to wonder why anyone would want to serve in such a position. Nevertheless, the system works quite well in giving a voice to the local community about the management of school affairs; however, from time to time some rather dubious individuals do manage to get themselves into positions of decision on the school board, particularly parents with a vendetta. These folks usually find that they can't affect very much because of the checks and balances that are in place, and the "characters" usually go away after one term. Upon being elected, members find that there are nuances, rules and regulations that abound in the operation of a school of which they aren't familiar. So when things are good, the Board lets the superintendent pull their strings; when things are bad they fire the superintendent, pay $80,000 for an outside agency to conduct a superintendent search and then hire another superintendent with less experience and pay him or her more money than the previous superintendent. Ultimately it comes back to letting the new superintendent pull their strings.

Back to the story, the scramble was on to check the rule book, to look at precedence, to discuss possible scenarios that could result and to talk to the school's legal counselor in order to come up with a plausible solution to carry the majority of the members while also appeasing the extreme factions on both sides of the issue. The superintendent, his inner sanctum and the Board's legal counsel pondered the resolution for quite a while and finally put its resolution on the agenda for the next school board meeting—it was starting to smell a little like last week's

James E. Billman

leftover catch of the day.

They met. They acknowledged the Concerned Citizens Committee. They went into closed session. They discussed. They discussed for over two hours and rendered their "decision." The Concerned Citizens Committee having grown tired of waiting had gone home. The decision was a true work of beauty. The student would not be expelled, however, she would not be allowed on any school property within the district to go to class or to take part in any school activity for the academic year. The school would provide her with a computer and the software so she could earn her credits via a virtual school.

Their decision showed compassion toward the offending student, and although the punishment may not have matched the crime in some people's estimation, it allowed the girl a chance to work it off and to redeem herself. Having been forced to miss the excitement and good times of the senior year was difficult for her and left a gap in her life, but it also allowed her to go forward positively at the time when she stood at a serious crossroad. In short, the decision endorsed by the majority of the members of the school board gave choice back to the girl. No one condoned what she did to her teacher, but no one condemned her forever after either. Everyone cheered when she graduated from college five years later. Good call.

The Board decision in this case did not repair the damage done to the teacher who was attacked. She was portrayed in the story to be a good teacher; she was obviously trying to teach on the day she was attacked, and at 40+ she was in it for the long haul. She knew the hazards of the occupation and she had been to the seminars on violence, but no one can stop a "sucker" punch, and it is very hard to act coherently when you're barely conscious. The teacher later found that she had many resources at her disposal and she used them. She also found a supportive faculty that rallied to her side and her star shone brightly in the eyes of her peers and students for years to come. And like many soldiers who have fought on the battlefield, she found an inner strength, a new level of consciousness if you will, and although never wishing to relive the experience, she came to believe that she was a better person for having endured it. She too, once stood at a crossroads and chose the high ground.

Lest we not forget the student who intervened and pulled the girl away from the teacher, you know—the unsung hero. Well, the school board had a special letter of commendation prepared for him signed by virtually everyone employed by the school that could write and added it to his official record and transcript. Whether it had anything to do with his subsequent scholarship to a prestigious Southern university or not, we can only speculate.

Sadly, it will happen again and we won't always be able to write happy endings.

I actually witnessed an attack on a teacher not unlike the one described above in 1950 when I was in third grade. Our teacher had been a victim of a childhood disease, probably polio, that made it very difficult for her to walk and perhaps affected her growth as she was also quite diminutive. She was attacked by the classroom bully when she insisted on something he didn't want to do, and was helped when another student came to her assistance. I remember that she remained in class for the rest of the day, week and year and carried on as if nothing had happened.

James E. Billman

Neither my classmates nor I thought much about it at the time, I suppose because she reacted the way she did in downplaying it all. I was too young to remember any of the ensuing effects of the confrontation, but I do remember very well that the boy was never allowed to return to school in any way, shape or form. He stayed in the community, but rather than stay in the third grade, went to work with his father and stayed in the business until his death. He never did have much contact with other people and few, if any, former classmates associated with him throughout our school days. Having no experience with him, I can't speak for him or his feelings on the matter.

Chapter 2: Schools

-1-

In the prologue, I was rather disdainful of educational research because of the way it relates to space and time in the same way that we'll never see a particular river again as it is moving past us while time is passing. Yes, it may seem like the same river and we may feel much the same way as the last time we saw the river, but technically it is not the same. Analogous to the flow of the river gradually downhill, I repeatedly contend that doing the same thing in education is not a viable approach because of the changes in society as well as the differences that permeate society today.

Continuing on the topic, research is a necessary tool, but it has to be scrutinized carefully and specifically to where it might apply. If a discipline program for the student body worked one place, that doesn't mean it works every place because schools are full of people who differ from each other. I once watched a discipline program work in the elementary school but fail miserably in the high school in the same community. We need a common sense and unified approach, and I write a lot about alignment in hoping to bring proscriptive approaches to the entire mess.

No researcher would say that the wording on a test used in 1934 would work equally well today. No researcher would agree that a study done in a borough of New York City applies to students in rural Minnesota. Shift happens. Few researchers would say a study done in rural Minnesota would also describe students in Minneapolis. However, researchers need to recognize that the defining numbers in Mrs. Jones 4th grade from 2008 will not reliably predict outcomes for 2009. It may not even come close. Why then are schools held accountable this year for what happened last year? Last year's class has moved on and they took their numbers with them so why wouldn't a specific grade's performance from their last testing period serve as a better indicator? Be proscriptive by looking ahead rather than prescriptive by looking back.

Time and space definitely warp outcomes. Research can be broad or very specific but it always misses time and space and therefore, the changes they bring. I'm talking about behavior and how different human beings change outcomes, not about the simple things that research and statistics do accurately measure and predict. Research done in 1934 on the mating habits of the tsetse fly is probably still valid. Statistical surveys that gather data in order to tell us who'll be our next president are quite reliable; so reliable in fact that it makes a person wonder why we even need to go through the motion of voting. Research done in nine schools in Milwaukee in 2006 does not tell us what will work in one school in Denver in 2008. Scientists know that a good experiment or research can measure only one variable at a time and educational research, working with many more than one variable, has not seemed to grasp this fact—plain and simple as it is.

Here is what I know. There are classes in the microcosm of a single school that are very good one year and not very good the next year. The same textbook is used, the same teacher delivers the content material following the same curriculum guide and the students are the brothers and sisters, the friends and relatives of the students in the class that did very well in the previous year. Teachers refer to this phenomenon as the class's "personality" and it is just one of those many things that happen when working with people. Maybe the peer leadership has a different orientation, maybe the mindset is different due to a new television program that "everyone" is watching, or maybe there were affecting sunspots throughout the year that the students in the class were conceived. Like the governing laws of nature, there are groups that don't conform to the norm just as no group *is* the norm.

-2-

And what is this norm, and how does this "normal" kid we know as a student fit?

There's a difference, however subtle, between normal and average. I called on Webster's Ninth New Collegiate Dictionary to show this difference. Both definitions are lengthy and get rather cumbersome so I include only what seems to be applicable. Normal is defined first of all as *a perpendicular to a line or a perpendicular to a tangent at the point of tangency.* Secondly, *it is according with, constituting, but not deviating from a norm, rule, or principle.* Later on in the list of definitions (#4)

James E. Billman

it says *of, relating to or characterized by average intelligence and development.* Average is defined thusly: *1. a single value that summarizes or represents the general significance of a set of values. 2. b. a level (as in intelligence) typical of a group, class or series.* The two aren't exactly interchangeable but are somewhat overlapping.

It's rather apparent that a normal student is going to come in around the fiftieth percentile on a standardized test and that the average *is* the fiftieth percentile, which is adjusted accordingly by the folks who assess the test. What a lot of people don't know is that the 50th percentile changes and has been sliding gradually down to accommodate the declining skills of students over the past twenty years. These same folks are pretty smart when dealing with numbers and have wisely stretched the normal a little bit to, say for the sake of the discussion, 10 percentage points on either side of the average number. This procedure makes sense and it doesn't raise the proverbial flags that parents sometimes wave when they see their kid may have fallen below the average because he or she can still be classified "normal." There are at least two reasons for 40-60 being the normal student range: 1) it appeases Mom and Dad and 2) testing agencies realize that students' scores undergo small fluctuations from time to time.

I find it humorous to note that the report from the school to the parents of the child in the 55th percentile would include the word "high" as in, "Your son Johnny tested in the high normal range." That sounds good. Conversely the same parents, had their daughter scored in the 40th percentile, would probably not hear, "Your daughter Sally tested in the low normal range," but rather, "Your daughter Sally tested normal for students her age."

That sounds good enough. With all good intentions we *can* make statistics work favorably for us and the school counselors and administrators have learned the tricks as well as anybody. Perhaps it would be more pertinent to say that school officials have become adept at averting certain things so they may appease parents, which brings the word *kowtow* to mind.

    I digress once again to another example from my experiences. To a school system, it's all about those nicely quantified numbers on the annual achievement batteries because a school's success or failure hinges on the outcome. Nobody in authority, and I mean nobody wants their school to be identified as being one in need of assistance because 1) it says that your school did not achieve the expected norm(s) and 2) your school is going to be invaded by the "experts." Experts being, in large part, teachers from the higher-achieving schools who are taken out of their classes and their schools to come and assist the school in need. I have always wondered why, beyond cultural differences from one place to another, that would be so bad because if a school really needs help, what's wrong with getting help? Anyway, it happened at this particular school where I was employed. We weren't really classified as being "in need" but we were close. (We were *almost* in need.) Our local chieftain rejected the numbers that were issued by the state and published in the newspaper—you know, just blatantly said the statistics weren't right. He and his army sharpened their pencils and went to work poring over the numbers and, by gosh, they did find a discrepancy in the way the results from the tests were compiled from one year to the next. It may have had the significance of a fly on an elephant but enough to save the day and raise the bar from "almost in need" to a school that "needs to be watched" or something just as ridiculous.

In using the word *batteries* in the above paragraph, that is exactly what the analysis of the standardized tests becomes. There are so many categories that fall under the scrutinizing eye of assessment that it is hard to imagine. They categorize performance by race, by family income, by student needs and even by attitude. The assessment team can even measure school and testing room intervention and they do exactly that because, as sad as it is, schools and teachers have been known to provide answers. This is a serious, very serious breach of professional ethics when this occurs.

So an average student is normal and a normal student is one whose score falls within a prescribed range on both sides of the annually-adjusted average. That makes it subtle enough for those who speak education-ese. Likewise, parents are pleased to hear that their child is normal and perhaps not so pleased to hear that their child is average simply because of the connotation between the two words. This is especially true because *smart parents generally have smart kids*. Of course if their child has a history of being low normal, it sounds better to be described as average.

The difficulty with average and normal is that some schools do not have an iota of a chance to attain these numbers. The unfortunate thing for these schools is that the experts and educational specialists knew that they were bound to fail when quantified nationally even before *No child left behind* was initiated. They were schools that had always had low numbers and NCLB wouldn't, couldn't and didn't make them raise their scores. Yet the program was implemented because it seemed good, noble and reasonable on the surface and appeared to be a way to measure achievement by quantification—just like a business and especially when endorsed by a no-nonsense education-oriented president.

Taking this notion of "average" a little farther shows the inapplicability of national rankings to measure or affect the influence of local flavor. It is not difficult to imagine that in a very economically poor school district with lots of in- and out-migration, with high unemployment rates for those of working ages (parents) and with a multitude of other societal problems that the average scores for a student from that district would not meet the average national scores. On the high end of the spectrum but in the same district, the academic leaders of a class may barely get into the 80th percentile on the national basis. Since the overall school scores are public information, the school bears the brunt of the criticism. But should it? One must refrain from taking a stereotypical approach at all costs but the children of the families who live in the district are the ones who populate the school for the most part. Whether rural or urban, sparsely or densely populated, these schools are not uncommon.

Who takes the blame? The school does. Who suffers the effects? The children do. Children simply are what they are and where they are by pure chance; they are children that have unfortunately been academically miscast by circumstance with nothing to say or do about it. This is apparent when these students with their numbers are compared to other children in other places with their numbers—both sets from the same scale. Educators have recognized this shortcoming and have addressed it prescriptively, but have done very little to change it with proscriptive measures because they are 1) hogtied with the system that is in place and too difficult to change and 2) wrapped around the contention that every child is entitled to an education that assumes parity. Number two is a tricky one because we interpret only one educational pathway to entitlement when, in truth, there are perhaps many tenable ways to reach objectives. Didn't the ancients say that all roads lead to Rome? I firmly believe that this can be fixed by placing students in realistic focus groups that are within their reach rather than placing all students on the same scale and holding them to standards and numbers that they cannot attain. This can be done through a standardized national curriculum

The last state that I taught in had addressed this in part by offering a menu of diplomas for a student to choose from. With parental assent, students would enroll in a course of study that matched their abilities and aspirations in life. I thought this was an example of some forward thinking that separated students into ability groups even though the program still required certain core classes and for students to show a certain level of proficiency in basic skills such as writing. It also allowed for students who may have difficulty in remaining in the honors program for example, to reset their goals in another diploma pursuit.

As previously indicated, standardized exams are a really big deal in the schools with which I am familiar, thanks in part to *No Child Left Behind* and state-mandated expectations . The administration tries to "pump up" the students to do their very best by hanging posters on the walls, offering rewards to a class for having "worked hard" on the testing days, and trying to make a student feel that with a little effort last year's chicken poop can become this year's chicken salad. The effort smacked of phoniness and the students were very adept at recognizing a hype job. I was told by the students in my homeroom that they would get their reward day or whatever just by (here we go again) "playing the game" because the administration has no way of knowing how hard they worked. "Keep your head down, don't get done too early and don't let the proctors walk by and notice a pattern of dots on your answer sheet," they told me. I taught science long enough to know that a serious approach on test day did not do much in raising a grade if the student hadn't put in the time doing the daily work, and I coached track long enough to know that just wanting to lower one's time or improve one's distance did not come from the mere desire to do it. So-called Field Days as rewards have become rather popular for having had a good test day; classes are canceled and the students get to go outside or to the gym and essentially play "grab ass" or just mill around in groups. I thought it was bad psychology on the school's part to try to make students feel that "just by trying" they could raise their scores from the previous year.

Another one of my schools got in the habit of having ice cream sundaes on Fridays for students who hadn't been a discipline problem throughout the week. To a good number of teachers, rewarding students for things that they should do anyway just didn't set too well with them. It asked me to step outside of my comfort zone, which was my classroom and to monitor students who couldn't conduct themselves reasonably if it only involved eating ice cream. I knowingly admitted to and often described myself as an old curmudgeon but these activities seemed counter-productive to those teachers who shared my opinion whereas many of the other teachers enjoyed them.

There were other negative outcomes from the standardized tests as a result of the administration's emphasis on their importance: the students got the impression that the school year was pretty much ended when the tests were finished. This happened in spite of the fact that virtually every student in the school knew that their achievement on the tests had nothing to do with anything individually reflective on them so why take them seriously. If a student had a grudge or didn't like the way he was treated, without accountability here was an opportunity to get back at the school. Students are weird sometimes and I'll focus a later chapter on the topic, but it's another example of the shift that I refer to quite often. I remember taking similar tests when in high school and they provided a scale by which we could compete with each other. I recently mentioned peer competition in a class that seemed to have little focus on anything academic and asked whether or not they had any competitive juices that flowed when they took tests. I got the answer to my question when a student remarked, "We aren't allowed to have juices in class." Speaking of accountability, schools are presently changing their thinking and asking colleges to include these scores in their selection processes for students; some have done this already.

Let me reiterate to make this perfectly clear. The measuring agencies assess a school's performance by the composite scores of the students on the standardized tests, but the students are not held accountable in any way, shape or form for their performance individually. Why? It would be so easy to incorporate a student's scores into his or her grades and so easy to put these scores on a transcript.

We know that a school is a non-entity. A school is composed of all those involved in it, both directly and indirectly; if you live in that school district, you are part of that school. A school is a pile of bricks, a shade tree on a hot day, the dinner table, and the street in the neighborhood—anywhere that communication can take place. Whatever the situation, the very presence of a school helps define an ecosystem and ecosystems are quite diverse places where informal and formal learning opportunities exist. I do not believe one set of quantified standards define average and normal chronologically-aged children from different human ecosystems. I do believe that national standards are fine, but they need to include more than mere tests to sort students accordingly; this can be done by delivering very similar curriculums to every student before they subject them to a standardized test.

-3-

Kindly indulge another sidebar example. People living in one place might measure length in feet whereas another group measures length in meters. Both systems serve the citizens equally well. A problem arises when these two populations start to interchange their business interests, their products and their sciences with each other. There's some confusion and certainly some reluctance for one group to learn the other, but once done, it really wasn't much of a problem of any great magnitude. Those who have no need to use both systems of measurement continue with the one that applies to them. Today there's no major concern anymore whether to use the metric or English systems of measurement—people just use the one that fits the need. Both systems are accepted. Although society hasn't attained concordance, the same thing is possible with cultures, language and, God forbid, religion.

A few years ago America was swept with a need to retool the way it did business and one of the catch phrases that arose was "quality management." America found that other foreign businesses, namely the automobile industry, were enjoying tremendous success in both producing a good product and showing profitability. They were not only cutting into the American manufacturer's market, they were kicking butt. Following this lead, American businesses pared wherever they thought it would be feasible to trim some fat, they overhauled their procedures and processes, they remodeled the way they did business to "think globally' and they quantified their self-assessment. Programs like ISO 9000 were designed to provide recognition and to facilitate doing business internationally as well as to make the operation of an organization more efficient. I had a part-time position with one company writing job descriptions and work procedures for employees as the company sought ISO certification, which was a permit that ensured that one business could do business with another ISO company in a glitch-free manner no matter where in the world each company might be. Doing business with an ISO 9000 organization assured the buyer of a quality product, and it allowed an organization to offer their products to customers on a world-wide scale.

Becoming global meant big change for virtually everyone in the world whether they recognized it or not. Businesses could relocate to where they could find an available, less costly labor force; money became interchangeable anywhere in the world;

Reform School

and being a small business meant that you were very, very likely to lose your livelihood if you didn't expand. Among other things, you would have to convert your measurements to the preferred metric system because it was "change or die" whether it seemed that way to you or not. Small farms, small towns and consequently small schools went the way of the albatross as once again, shift happened. With bigger, more efficient and certainly more expensive machinery, John Deere™ killed the small farmer in America. Next, John Deere made bigger and better high-quality machinery that didn't wear out quickly and sold them to the large farmer. After equipping the large farmers in America, John Deere ultimately went global. As a gesture of friendship to its customers, but also as an attempt to stay alive during the down turn of the eighties, John Deere started selling insurance, clothes and toys, maybe even potato chips.

    The organizational management aspect of the movement was of interest to me because it suggested to management that it should let the workers get more involved in optimization of the processes that brought about the product. Successful organizations had realized that there were other ways to increase output than by hollering "faster" and/or putting line employees on piecework. Organizational management welcomed everyone in the organization to input the processes and the procedures involved in making the product. Everything from paperwork to cleanup was fair game for scrutiny as the concept of management went from "me" to "we."

    At the time, a forward-thinking dean of the technical college where I taught believed the same thing could be done in our school. His reasoning was solid; our product at the college was to supply qualified graduates in electronics, computer maintenance, electro-optics, robotics and other technical occupations to organizations that were doing business globally. Further, if the college did their business this way and if teachers were versed in quality management procedures, then students would be better prepared to get jobs. I bought into the concept whole-heartedly and, having experience with ISO 9000, volunteered for the implementation team and co-chaired the ad hoc committee. It just didn't go the way we thought it would and not much ever came out of either the Dean's or the committee's efforts. Whether the committee was too far from management, whether the Dean expected more than he got from us or whether other things became more important, we felt no impact as a result of our work and interest dwindled. Community colleges are very dynamic and leadership positions are revolving doors; those of us on the committee also thought that our lack of getting the program off the ground had much to do with concurrent things like departmental changes and internal leadership. It was unfortunately an ill-timed effort.

This was also the time when computers were marrying robots and bringing a new age of Computer Numerical Control (CNC) operations to business and industry. CNC suggested a beautiful concept that would take the workers away from doing repetitive menial tasks and let them work in jobs of higher technology—that is if the worker was capable of working in higher technology. The fact that there would be far fewer workers was made quite evident in practicality; hence, the death of industry as we knew it in the United States.

The concept of quality management honed the operations

of businesses all over the globe, so why not put the same concepts to work for the schools? Most of us know that schools have business managers, they undergo audits and have operating budgets all of which make them appear to be a business. Most of us also know that a large percentage, as high as 90%, of the money a school receives goes to salaries for employees such as teachers, administrators and support staff. But is a school a business that can be organizationally managed?

Considering a K-12 school as a business is a little befuddling when thinking in terms of manufacturing a product and delivering it to its customers. If schools are businesses then students are the raw material, and competent students (remodeled students?) are the products to be delivered to the consumers. I cannot think that K-12 students are products in the manner that business identifies its products. So who are the customers of the schools if not the members of the very society that the students live in? A school takes in children, runs them through the mechanism and turns them out into the environmental ecosystem from which they came. Are the students truly better for having gone through local societal processing? Do they now have more opportunity to compete in a market that has become global? Absolutely not. Are our school leaders who act locally, really thinking globally? Considering the way schools are tradition-bound, I have sincere doubts.

I have mentioned that some schools, as they are structured today, do not have a chance to attain average numbers. The sad thing is that the experts and educational specialists knew this before *No child left behind* was initiated yet it was implemented because it seemed reasonable on the surface and appeared to be

James E. Billman

a way to measure achievement by quantification—just like a business.

A K-12 school is all about human beings, not widgets, automobiles or green vegetables, which is the primary reason why a K-12 school cannot be operated like a business. The raw material is theoretically molded and transformed into the finished product, a diverse, multi-faceted human being who is already a product of his environment. When students from similar environments are summarily lumped together they can be quantified and the quantification does give us an overall picture that is both 1) comparable to previous years and 2) can possibly serve as a predictor for future years. That is, if the same things are measured each year. Because the big picture is so big, it doesn't speak to an individual, his school and sometimes not even his state. Students aren't beans in a can or Toyota Corollas rolling off an assembly line and can't be quantified the same way. In short, a K-12 school is different than a business and a school cannot be operated in the future the same way it is structured at present. So we need to change our schools. We need to go global.

Turn the situation around and let's put some quality management theory into a school situation. Archie® and Jughead® are classmates. Archie could be a better student than he demonstrates, but there are so many activities such as sports, a part-time job, and of course, Veronica® and Betty® to distract him. Jughead is the class clown, a slacker and a cut-up in class, that is, when he's awake. All the students think him to be funny and Jughead feeds on their attention. Archie manages to earn mostly B's and scores in the mid-eighties on standardized tests

Reform School

whereas Jughead gets low D's and scores consistently below the 10th percentile. None of the teachers will fail him and run the risk of having him in their class again next year. If K-12 was a business, Archie would be a typical product and they would put him in the can with the rest of the similarly judged beans or he would be sent out to the car dealership as a quality-checked automobile—depending how we view this Archie-as-product. (The automobile Archie, however, doesn't meet global standards.) Business, on the other hand, would also put Jughead in a can—the trash can. That is the succinct difference between business and the K-12 school system.

A school operating under the auspices that everyone has a right to "get an education" turns its focus on Jughead in hopes that he can be made into a contributing member of society, whatever that means beyond sounding noble. The school also makes the assumption that Archie is in good shape, just look at his scores so the school says "Let's leave him where he is because he'll take care of himself." That, in a nutshell, is the mantra of *No Child Left Behind*.

Two points I'd make from this: 1) A lot more money will be spent in turning Jughead around than by eliminating Jughead and thereby enabling the school to raise the bar for Archie, and 2) you might recall that Archie and Jughead live in Riverdale®, a small rural town most likely to presently be in decline. Without many global prospects, about all the school can do is to try to prepare its students to leave town because there are just no jobs to keep them home. Jughead, in essence doesn't have the capability to leave town because he has spent his time in school screwing around in the academic classes rather than receiving job training in areas where he might succeed. Jughead has no job and no prospects because, if nothing else, his reputation precedes him. Conversely, Archie hasn't been prepared adequately to compete globally because old Jughead's antics proved to be a deterrent to everyone in his class. And as unfortunate as it is, Archie didn't have the wherewithal to think that he was being robbed of the education he needed to compete by Jughead's behavior.

Much of the thinking of the educational experts actually inhibits its charges—the students. School officials need to think globally and work together in building a functional global curriculum. Actually there are a few international preparatory school courses of study, but they are often thought of as not being "American" enough by people who don't really understand the purpose or intent of them. Another issue that meets resistance is that some folks think global education to be exclusionary because of its rigorous nature by the fact that it doesn't allow for mainstreaming. And some people will never agree with my notion that being able to go to school should be an earned privilege. It's a tough sell but my feelings are that under the present structure mainstreaming is detrimental to the quality of the graduates. We need to think in terms of the "greater good" when establishing educational guidelines.

I reiterate once more, the emphasis of my entire argument in this book is based on the contention that K-12 schools must be perceived, recognized, and operated as a privilege for those who have earned the right to attend it.

Let me talk in terms of dollars and cents. K-12 schools receive funding from local, state and federal sources with the least amount coming from the federal government. In fact there are quite a few occasions when what is allocated for school support doesn't match what actually gets written on the check because it is preempted by higher-priority items. Budgets must be balanced but promises aren't always kept and consequently, what is promised is not necessarily delivered. Again, shift happens. Both state and federal governments project what they are going to allocate yet there always seems to be more that goes out than is comes in—no big news on that front.

As said previously, a person has knowledge of that which he or she is closest to or has experienced, but it seems that a cost breakdown per student in the K-12 schools where I was employed is in the neighborhood of $5000 per year. To operate, a school needs $5000 per student per year so in my hypothetical group of 27 students in Mrs. Jones' room, that totals $135,000 of which Mrs. Jones might get $45,000 or 1/3 of the money generated as her salary. For Mrs. Jones, this amounts to very close to $1.50/ hour per child for six hours a day for 180 days per year. ($43,740/year) However, many teacher contracts call for a 190 day contract and some are moving to a 240 day work year for teachers. During their workday, teachers are assigned extra duties and promised (but rarely delivered in entirety) a duty-free preparatory period where they must be available for more extraneous demands and/or are expected to work on school things. Further if the mandatory in-service days, required professional training days and the trimmed-down holidays would be included in the $1.50/hour per student for a (preparatory period included) seven hour day, the annual salary of Mrs. Jones would soar to a heftier $53,875. Teacher negotiating committees sometimes use this tactic when bargaining for the next year's contract.

"Oh please Mr. and Mrs. School Board Member, just give us a reasonable baby-sitting wage, or how about only a dime an hour per student? Who would rue a hard-working teacher a dime?" A dime would mean an annual raise of $3591. However, the school board would look upon this request as a 6.67% raise, and that would be a preposterous amount for a publicly-employed teacher.

Here's some more fun with numbers. One of the school districts that I taught at had approximately 8000 students and 450 certified teachers, which would be a student to teacher ratio of around 18:1. Another school district where I taught at had roughly 700 students and 30 certified teachers for a ratio of 23:1. Both schools were then and still are severely strapped financially.

The larger school had one superintendent, 3 assistant superintendents and approximately 70 additional employees at the central office of which 5 of the 70 warranted having their pictures on the district website, if that was an indication of importance. This represents one central office employee for every six teachers (74:450). The smaller school had one superintendent and 2.5 others in the central office (I'm including the head of transportation as the 0.5). The smaller school's ratio of central office people to teachers would be one to 8.6 (3.5:30).

Further, using close approximations the large school district had 18 principals and assistant principals, 15 guidance counselors and at least 35 full time support employees that were not certified teachers. If these folks are added to the non-teacher—teacher ratio from above, it goes to ~ 142:450 or one support person for every 3.2 teachers. The small school, on the other hand has two principals, two guidance counselors and five full-time support employees, which bring the ratio to 12.5:30 or one support staffer for every 2.4 teachers.

Based solely on the ratios, one could make a fairly sound contention that the larger school has more central office specialists breathing down the teacher's neck and fewer support people to help the teacher. Having taught in both systems, I don't need numbers to concur that the large school with almost 1.5 times more people in the central office per classroom teacher is top-heavy. A basic tenet in *Business 101* teaches students that the older an organization is, the more top-heavy it becomes. Heck, we all know what too many cooks do to the broth.

The data I presented also says that the large school has one central office employee for every 108 students, and the small school has one central office person for every 200 students. Whether a person sees this as twisting the numbers or not, the rather obvious conclusion is that the larger school isn't being run with the same efficiency as the smaller school. Some statistic-skewing factors that call for a larger central office would be things such as the ethnicity of the local population, the meddlesome nature of the state as my two comparisons were in two different states, and the simple facts that a larger school has more program diversity and more physical structures so there is more to go wrong. For example, the larger school has 2500 air conditioners as reported in the local paper, whereas the smaller school in my comparison has less than ten, none of which are in a classroom. It is worthy to note that both of the schools chosen for comparison are in economically depressed areas and that they do compare favorably on national student achievement batteries.

I find it rather impressive to think that if the thirteen upper-echelon employees from the bigger school district would pile into a small school bus to go to a meeting at the state capitol, they would represent nearly 1.5 megabucks in annual salary, whereas if the same thing was done in the small district, the superintendent who is also the curriculum director and represents less than 1.5 kilo bucks per year. Assuming that each superintendent earns the same amount, that's a big difference, even spread over 12 people. There are two sides to the issue so draw your own conclusions concerning the "fat" in school management. I guess knowing what many CEO's of major companies earn; educational managers must feel somewhat short-changed at times. Whereas many officers in the armed forces are personally responsible for millions of dollars of equipment yet are paid less than school administrators

'Nuff said about management.

-5-

Community and Junior colleges generally find themselves holding the short straw when it comes to money so they have to scramble to make ends meet. 1) They don't generate much interest in the research area because they don't have a renown staff rife with PhD's, 2) academically they are a prep school and not high on the list for gifts from graduates who have done well financially, 3) their state funding formulas often aren't favorable and 4) their main selling point is based on low tuition. A serious rap on community college technical programs is that a person goes to school to learn a trade that won't support him or her. Although the academic classes are guaranteed to articulate with same-state colleges and universities, students often find that the level of the class is somewhat different and requires the transferring community college student to re-take a similarly-named class. Take calculus for example. The community college offers calculus and a student takes the class and does well in it. When the student decides to enroll in the engineering program at a state university, yes the hours transfer and the student receives credit, but the class at the university is called *"Calculus for Engineering I,"* and alas, the transferring student did not have that actual class and really only gets the credit hours and the benefit of some repetition and overlap that would probably help him or her perform better in *Calculus for Engineering I."* Another problem the transferring student might find is that there is most likely a calculus sequence required to complete the engineering program, *"Calculus for Engineering I, II and often III."* Even if given credit for *I* on transferring, the student may find himself lost if enrolled into *II*.

    So the community and junior college has to do other things to keep their doors open, most of which are good and noble. They have economic development departments, they have grant writers that come up with some really off the wall stuff, they articulate with area business and industry in training their new employees as well as re-certifying old employees, they offer programs that reach out and teach the local citizenry quality management, they offer advisement to business, they offer academic and technical classes to high schools, sponsor school-to-work programs, offer general interest courses and limit themselves only by their own imaginations. The greatest thing their programs do is that they serve their local constituency with truly a global perspective.

As mentioned, my best memories concerning educational experiences came as part of a grant program at a community college when I was hired to be the coordinator/lead instructor for a federally funded demonstration grant designed to "put women and people of minorities into positions of high technology" (the way things were said in 1989). This was an 18 month program that included recruitment of area women who would like to learn and get involved in technical positions as well as a second segment that co-opted with an electrical union to teach apprentice electricians basic electronics. We recruited the women, and offered alternative delivery for five evenings a week for an academic year teaching everything from Mathematics for Electronics to Laboratory Instrumentation and Measurement. One hundred and thirty five showed interest in the program, 30+ women started it and 17 actually graduated. It was rigorous and demanding, mostly because of the time frame. Knowing that a good portion of the women had full-time day jobs, the program started at five in the afternoon and went until ten in the evening. The union electrical workers went to school on Friday evenings for five hours and for a full day on Saturday in addition to being full time employees for their respective electrical firms. None of the participants were paid but the training and all the textbooks were without fee. The men had a harder time than the women primarily because of the pertinence of the instruction compared to what the students perceived to be of value to them. In other words the carrot at the end of the stick was more appealing to the women.

The crux of the story is that the men who successfully completed the program were in the same job position as before and although the women were given the benefit of the college's placement services, they really weren't specifically trained for any skilled positions in the field. The women consequently were urged to continue in one of the school's five different departments of high technology that existed at the time, or they could enroll in the follow-up grant program designed to prepare them as micro-computer specialists—also offered as an alternate delivery (odd hours) program. The bottom line was that it did generate some good money for the school and the participants graduated with the then-marketable skill of being more computers knowledgeable. Targeted areas of recruitment spoke to single mothers and women who had earned a GED and these ladies, for the most part, needed to work to support their families.

Community colleges truly look at themselves as a business entity in the community. Many are called "Area" community colleges and they target students to enter programs that are in their geographical area and don't profess to be something that they aren't. By this I mean they don't promise enrollees in the Culinary Arts program that they are going to get positions as chefs in the Waldorf-Astoria, but the school does prepare one to work in good restaurants and institutions. Diesel mechanics may not know their job any better than someone who received on-the-job-training, but the former has a certificate that substantiates that they completed the program and met the criteria required by the school. That little piece of paper that signifies completion means a lot, as we all know.

As previously stated, community colleges have also addressed the issue of doing business globally and they did it quite a while ago—even before it was either popular or necessary. The technical end of most community colleges works hard to develop a reputation for placement of their graduates. After all, the students came to the program so they could get a job when it was over—community college technical programs are focused on jobs, not the arts. To address this necessary issue, technical schools have advisory boards staffed by outside people in business and industry that meet periodically to discuss whether or not the school is delivering graduates to their sectors who can function with a minimum of further training. Advisory Board members are often from the business sectors and the actual business that hire the graduates so it becomes dynamically win-win; as the businesses change so do the preparatory programs of the technical colleges. And the beautiful part is that as the businesses and industries that hire the area graduates "go global" in their operations, so does the curriculum of the technical school. The student is empowered. There is no greater word in all of education than "empowering" a student! I bring this into my discourse because these technical programs could just as well serve that population of current high school students who are "ready" to learn a skill and go to work. Those students, in other words, who want to get into the real world.

Colleges, both junior and senior, can operate as businesses because they charge their "customers" to get in the door and provide a commodity in return. What the person does with the commodity is up to each individual. You don't have to graduate, you don't have to stay, you can study or not study—it's very much a business-like arrangement. K-12 students do have to stay in school whether they pass or fail or until they reach a certain age, and in many cases because students do have to stay, they disrupt those other students around them and bring havoc to the entire process. There isn't very much that is business-like at all in public education. In college, if you don't utilize the commodity, you're out; in K-12, if you don't utilize the commodity, you get special attention while you hold back the rest of the class. And the worst part of the K-12 arrangement is that the student not making use of the commodity provided isn't taken out of it and put in a program that would be meaningful and useful to them in the future.

-6-

In discussing schools, it seems appropriate to look historically at the changes that the global movement has necessitated; changes that directly or indirectly have rocked many of us to the very foundation of our existence. Change may seem gradual in terms of historic eras, but quite rapid in terms of individual human life spans.

I feel that the size of a school affects its ability to deliver quality education. My discussion focus on K-12 schools and once again, my experiences in these schools is at the senior high school level. Throughout I make the allusion that teachers feel that a better learning environment exists in a smaller class; I know I felt this way. When having a positive informal learning atmosphere in addition to a smaller teacher-pupil ratio, the stage is set for communication—it can't get any better than that. Essentially, that is the formula for successful home schooling, and as the results indicate, kids that are home schooled tend to score higher on standardized exams than kids who are enrolled in public school. But the extremely small size of the home school can only take some of the credit for success because much of it once again comes back to the tendency for *smart parents to have*...you know the rest.

I prefer small schools. Obviously legislators prefer the schools in the districts they represent. Regents and appointed state educational board officials, who are often successful businesspersons, prefer larger schools, and it is these officials who have the most say-sos in the issue. Consequently the states that have a large rural contingency have had some pretty embittered battles waged over consolidation of small schools into larger schools.

Historically, when a small town loses its high school, the locals view it as another nail in the coffin that is their town; however, if the town wasn't already in decline in the first place there would be no consolidation necessary. There have been some fairly monumental disagreements concerning where the consolidated school will actually go, especially when old rivals consolidate or when all the population centers involved in the consolidation umbrella are so small they can hardly keep their own post office. Most of the arguments boil down to "My town is less in decline than your town," so consequently there are quite a few consolidated school districts in Iowa, for example, that ended up being built out in the middle of what had been a corn field. (Good for rising transportation costs, huh?) Originally schools from each town fought each other on the football field and basketball court; they fought the Department of Education to not consolidate them; they fought about the location(s); and they fought about their new name. At present some Iowa schools have consolidated twice and consequently have gone through the whole process again.

It might be better to say that consolidation came about in a sequence. First, families got smaller because John Deere got bigger; secondly, small towns got smaller because Wal-Mart™ got bigger; and thirdly, the schools got smaller and couldn't generate the funds necessary for mandated programs and courses, which is a story all its own. Don't get me wrong, John Deere and Wal-Mart are successful examples rather than culprits because they recognized how to morph in a modern society. The culprits are those who couldn't think globally in the face of change— they committed community suicide. No, don't blame the tall dogs but rather the short dogs that couldn't see over the grass in front of them. Cases in point are the thriving small colleges in rural settings who had visionary leadership that enabled them to make the transition from local to global vs. the colleges who have closed their doors over the past thirty years.

-7-

The themes of this chapter have been to compare and contrast schools; schools and businesses; and high schools and colleges. I once again expounded on the importance of quantification, but have found it rather difficult to agree that the same percentiles describe diverse settings. I expressed my displeasure concerning mainstreaming all children together and attempted to make the point that it restricts the better students who need to get even better so that they can compete on a global level. In having been an avid reader of Archie Comics®, I know that Jughead was more of a latent genius than the way I depicted him, but the name struck me as I wrote the analogy. I fully realize that there are exceptions to every example I cite and every argument I offer; of course there are because schools work with people using other people called teachers. I argued that because of the wide range of human conditions and mindsets we need to scrutinize both research and statistics when we compare them to our particular set of circumstances. I remain convinced, however, that schools are not serving their constituency adequately because they are 1) too wishy-washy in making students earn their right to be there, and 2) they are not thinking globally.

Reform School

Real Life Adventure #2

The school was staid Midwest. It had consolidated in the first wave that crossed the state in the 1960's as the school board members recognized that things weren't going to get better as state mandates made it more and more difficult for smaller schools. New funding formulas made it very hard to operate in lesser-populated districts, there were requirements for a larger selection of classes and it was virtually impossible to attract qualified teachers willing to make a commitment to a fading rural community. The proverbial handwriting was on the wall with two old school buildings in two small towns, each of which could barely total 1500 citizens so the decision to merge was made easier. Approximately seven miles apart, it also made a lot of sense to buy some land and build a larger school that would offer more "opportunities" to the students. Although no one said it aloud, opportunities actually meant that there would be more ways for the students to leave their communities after graduation. Depending on the route taken, both towns were within twenty miles of a small city of 50,000, which also expedited the decision lest they would eventually be gobbled up by the city school. They concurred, "Too far to bus our kids."

There were issues, of course. Old sports rivalries, independence, autonomy and identity all had to be reconciled into a new singularity. "There goes our town," many of the citizens murmured, not realizing that it was in fact the opposite way around; the school was the victim of the declining townships For all the difficulties this new district suffered, they were comparatively mild in the face of some other districts in the state facing similar circumstances.

Today, not much has changed regarding the populations of the communities. The area is still rural but with far fewer people living outside the city limits of the two towns. With a bane turned to blessing, both communities found their continued existence tied to the industry of the nearby city that enabled a daily work commute, which also made each town appealing as bedroom communities. Fewer farmers meant fewer business owners, and since many of the residents now traveled to the city where they found work, they also shopped in the big box stores. In addition, each town held onto a few cottage industries that remained fairly stable and employed approximately 40 people. The demographics, however, have changed considerably through the years following consolidation.

Actually the school merger galvanized the two communities and was the single best reason for the constancy of the population of the two towns. The proximity to the city and its amenities made the school attractive to teachers who could enjoy their anonymity away from the school if they chose to commute. There was now a nice, modern facility that, by doubling its enrollment, could afford to offer competitive salaries to the faculty. Also, the reputation connecting good standardized test

Reform School

scores with Midwestern rural schools made either town a good place to raise a family. That matters would work out the way they did in this instance was exceptional.

Today, over 40 years later, the school population hasn't changed much; it is still predominately Caucasian with never more than five African-American students at any given time but experiencing a growing Hispanic contingent due to a processing plant in the nearby city. The graduating senior class averages around 75 students. High school sports and activities are the mainstay of community activities with many parents attending every event their children are involved in.

In 1998, the long-standing principal retired and a gentleman who had been an assistant principal at a Wisconsin high school seemed to be a solid candidate and was offered the position. He accepted. As most administrators have a tendency to do, some changes had to be made so the new principal could impact his presence. Good or bad, the new mandates weren't very well received by either the staff or the students. No hats in the building, all teachers will be present in the hallways between classes, all male students will wear belts and have their shirts tucked in, and on and on. Teachers were given pedagogical books to read, were tested on the material in the books and were mandated to attend discussion groups. Students had their lockers and personal vehicles searched for contraband and weaponry. By the end of the school year the public outcry was sufficient for the school board to not renew his contract citing that the abruptness of his manner contributed to his unpopularity. No one in the community took the time to follow Principal "Al Catraz's" career after the close of the school year.

James E. Billman

The next principal was "more suited" to the environment and atmosphere of a rural setting. A former social studies teacher who had gone to school in the summers to gain administrative certification, he had most recently been in the northern part of the state and was hoping to get a position a little bit closer to his son and family. An older gentleman, he assured the Board that he was not a "climber" and had no intentions of doing anything but making this area his home. His record was solid and he offered glowing recommendations; he was unanimously voted by the Board to be the man to fill the vacancy.

Again change was affected and on the first day of school at the all-grade assembly the new principal read the rules as he had amended them and the school year got off to a good start. Incidentally, the first day is always a good day as students and teachers "feel" each other out. In fact the entire year went pretty well with only a few infractions that were handled quickly and efficiently according to the rules. As the school year drew to a close, everybody loosened up a little bit; after all, this was a small school and everybody knew everybody else.

The following year started off much like the previous year ended. Students were relaxed, teachers friendly and outwardly helpful. The football team won the conference and went to the state tournament for the first time in four years. Both the boys' and the girls' basketball teams were primed for a good season so community support was excellent. A person measuring sound intensity might have noticed a slight rise in the noise in the hallways, and if something wasn't good, it usually came from the band room corridor. One girl had been pushed into the boys' restroom and had cut her lip badly enough to need a few stitches.

Reform School

There were some allegations that she had been groped at the time, but there were no official complaints filed. The band teacher had resigned prior to the incident and probably hadn't been vigilant in her duties to maintain order in the hallways.

The third year brought the "same old, same old." Students who had been freshmen when the principal started were now juniors and the sophomores were seniors. Some of the teachers were noticeably a bit more lax in their duties and in the teacher meetings on Tuesday mornings; the principal sometimes had to remind the faculty to keep their guards up and stick to the rules. That year brought a new band director, math teacher and art teacher. The seniors of that year were a rather rambunctious group and there were a few incidents of misbehavior that called for some three-day expulsions. One of the business teachers married her former student, a senior from two years ago, so the rumors flew over how they might have become so cozy with each other. A boy and girl got caught in a school bus after hours in a state of undress and a freshman boy was seen urinating in the water fountain. The halls were more rowdy than the previous year and the decibel level went up again. The senior prank for the year was the release of a 100 pound shoat that had somehow been captured and released in the school during the previous evening.

By the fourth year, it was known that the principal was indeed a mellow fellow. Students sent to the office for disciplinary reasons were often sent back to the same classroom that same period. Rather than punishing offenders of the rules, students were put on their own recognizance to not repeat the offense. Teachers continued to be held to the rules with only gentle reminders in teacher meetings yet no teacher was singled out for not doing his/her job. The physics teacher caught three students sharing a copy of a pornographic magazine during a laboratory exercise that had been stashed inside a physics book. There were some mumblings in the communities about the lack of discipline at the high school that came to a boil when the new art teacher was discovered to be hosting a party with some senior boys in attendance. Of course there was alcohol involved and by now the in-school incidents were growing to be too numerous to list.

    The next year brought a discussion among the board members that something had to be done regarding the overall behavior of the students; there were too many reports of misbehavior reaching the members of the school board. The principal was quizzed about the situation and agreed to crack down on the offenders and made the suggestion that perhaps a dean of students would be a good idea. In recommending the football coach/athletic director he pointed out that enrollment was down slightly and other classes could absorb the coach's teaching load. It became a done deal with the understanding that the dean of students would handle the day-to-day disciplinary issues and the principal would take care of the more serious cases referred to him. The principal was also due to reach retirement age in March of the school year.

    By now there were several incidents of fighting in the school. Teachers were getting cussed out by students, infractions had become pretty rampant and punishments remained minimal. It was no longer an atmosphere where the friendly teacher went out of the way to be helpful, but one in which some formerly diligent teachers were reluctant to go out into the hallways and do their job because other teachers blatantly ignored theirs. Being a teacher himself, the dean of students neither had authority to bring another teacher into tow nor cherished becoming alienated from his colleagues. The principal became a recluse and most of the time the door to his office was closed. His attendance record had gotten progressively worse each year that he had been at the school, and he missed over thirty days in his fifth year. He still was the same easy-going, friendly individual that he had always been, but was dissociated with so many of the problems that existed. The Board instituted "Saturday School," for repeated offenders, and a new staff position was created to monitor an in-school suspension room. Both the Saturday school and the in-school suspension rooms came to be regarded as prestigious by the students. One teacher was heard to remark that "the animals had taken over the zoo," and by the end of the school year, six teachers resigned, as did the principal.

With matters in a true state of turmoil, change was imminent if order was ever going to be restored. Complaints were coming in to the superintendent, and the school board members had also fielded their share of the same. The football coach was returned to the classroom but was paid extra to double up on his athletic director duties and still be a presence in the hallways and restrooms. Some feared that a Resource Officer might be needed and a cost estimate was solicited from the Sheriff's Department. Slowly the certified positions got filled for the start of another school year.

School started with some real apprehension on the part of all those who hailed from the two communities who spoke

James E. Billman

for education. As per protocol, the new principal found himself addressing the faculty, who sat together in a clump and the student body who filled the bleachers. At the very top of the bleachers were the "bad asses" sprawling with their seed corn hats on their heads, and protruding lower lips stuffed with "chew." "New principal means no rules and no one ain't told us nothin' yet."

    Something that had evolved in the five years with the former principal in this district was that some of the farm boys, called Ag kids, weren't farm kids at all but they portrayed the impression of knowing much more about farming than any school-trained agriculture teacher. There's an old saying among educators about "expelling a troublesome student to the shop," meaning that if a student is in the manual shop classes and/or the agriculture areas of the school he or she is out of the way. In this particular school, as in others, these groups manage to manipulate their schedules to spend 80% of the day in the shop area taking classes such as Woodworking I, II, III, and IV, Building Trades, Crop Management, and the all-time favorite, Welding. There is quite a menu from which they can choose, mostly as an accommodation to keep them away from the general student population. After five years of riding roughshod with the same principal and after running out three Voc Ag teachers during those years, these "knuckle-draggers" thought they ruled the roost. Generally ungoverned and specifically undisciplined, this little band of boys could often be found doing all sorts of things contrary to the operation of an orderly school day.

    There had been an incident during the past year when the agriculture teacher had been hit in the back of the head with a "C" battery thrown at him. Although the incident happened in a classroom setting, the "student code of silence" prevented anyone from seeing who actually threw the battery. The teacher was visibly hurt and had to be taken to the Emergency Room at the hospital in the city, and many of the faculty members thought that the principal did not pursue the guilty party with enough zeal because everyone else in the school knew who the battery pitcher was.

The new principal, to say the least, had a monumental task in front of him as he faced the student body. The Board had found his credentials good; he had met with the teachers during the previous workshop days but was certainly an unknown quantity in the eyes of the community. The final bell rang to signal the start of first period amid a buzz that continued. Precisely one minute after the bell whether prompted or spontaneous, every teacher arose and, as quickly as they could, spread themselves throughout the bleachers to shush the students—it had to have been an orchestrated action the way it was played out.

Order was restored except at the very top of the bleachers where the five self-proclaimed very tough farm boys sat with their hats still on their heads and laughing at the difficulty one fairly corpulent teacher had had in climbing onto the bleachers and nestling herself among the students. No teacher had dared come into their domain. The new principal began by welcoming everyone for the start of the school year and telling them his name. In continuing, he made no allusion to the way things had been or to the fact that there was going to be some necessary changes made. He explained the bell schedule and how the split lunch period worked for the benefit of the freshmen and new students. He explained student's rights as far as locker searches, bullying incidents, student right to due process and he mentioned that all this information was also outlined in the student planners of which each student would soon be given in their homeroom. These were necessary items that he had to do. So far, the boys at the top of the bleachers hadn't given the principal his due as they continued to talk and laugh among themselves. When one of boys pushed another which elicited a shove back, the principal stopped his speech, looked in their direction and asked politely if they would please pay attention to what he was saying. "And would you please remove your hats when you are in the school building?"

These guys didn't like being singled out but nevertheless slowly complied; a couple of them gave the principal "the sneer." You know, the one that emanates utter revulsion as well as characterizing the scorn that only teenage rebelliousness can typify. Next, the principal introduced the teachers that were returning and followed up with the new teachers and their subject areas. In introducing the new English teacher, one of the boys in the top row gave a wolf whistle to the amusement of the student body and followed with the comment "I'd sure like to get a piece of her class," loud enough for most everyone within thirty feet of him to hear.

The principal did not hesitate but marched up the aisle of the bleachers, grabbed the offending student in a vice-like grip by the ear and pulled him to his feet. Still leading the surprised student by the ear they went back down to the gym floor whereupon the student tried to shake himself free. It was the ultimate embarrassment to be humiliated like this in front of everyone; no way would the principal get away with this. "Let

Reform School

go, you son of a bitch!"

No more had the word "bitch" got out of the kid's mouth when the principal turned toward the tough boy and with one swoop kicked both feet out from under him, which caused the kid to fall forward and find himself face down on the floor with the wind knocked out of him. The principal promptly pulled the kid to his feet, spun him around and grabbed him by the seat of his jeans with one hand and the back of the kid's shirt with the other hand. Next, he lifted the kid to the point that only his toes were able to touch the floor, a move that rendered the kid unable to control what was happening and literally took him out of the gymnasium, through the vestibule and to the front door of the school. In the total silence of the gym the principal was heard to say, "Out! And don't come back."

Re-entering the gym, marching up the aisle to the four remaining now not-so-tough boys who were sitting on razor blades, the principal pointed to each one of them in turn and told them they had three days suspension and that each of them should report to his office no later than 0745 the following Monday with a parent or guardian. "And give me your hats." He stood in the aisle with four seed corn hats in his hand as the deposed students got out of their seats and wordlessly left the building. Returning to the podium, the principal introduced the remaining two new teachers.

"Do you have any questions?" he asked the rest of the students.

There were none. "If not, be sure that you read and heed to the exact letter the rules of this school as explained in your Planners. I want each and every one of you to have a good school year, study hard and have as much fun as you can within the rules. You may now proceed to First Period."

Three of the four students who had been given the three day suspension reported as instructed the following Monday. They were given their Planner Books and the principal read the rules while the students followed and the parents listened. Again, were there any questions? "Do you understand that with all your rights you do not have a right to distract other students from being able to exercise their rights? School is an earned privilege and you earn that right by following the rules."

Looking each parent in turn in the eyes, he asked if any of them had any questions or comments to which each answered in the negative. "Each of us in this room has a responsibility to these young men in giving them the leadership, discipline and guidance necessary to make them contributing members of society. It is a serious obligation that binds us all together." Finally the principal told the boys that they would get their hats back at the end of the term and that as of this moment they had paid for their infraction. The only remaining thing was that each of them had missed three days' work that would have to be made up.

The parents of the boy that was permanently expelled as well as the mother of the boy who did not come to the Monday morning meeting petitioned the school board and got on the agenda of the next meeting. They brought an attorney from the city that presented a plea for reinstatement of their children and called for "the immediate dismissal of the principal for his participation in harsh and unfair treatment that brought undue embarrassment, physical abuse and public ridicule to two citizens of our community."

    The Board went into a closed session to discuss the issue and thirty minutes later came back and told the complainants that the boy given the three day suspension could re-enter school at the start of the next semester or he could enroll in the alternative school right away. The other boy was told that his only option was to enroll at the alternative school, but he would have to wait until the start of next semester. And of course, both boys could seek enrollment to another school outside of the district. The lawyer sputtered about a law suit in appeal and liberally used the word "sue" on several occasions, but to date nothing has been done.

James E. Billman

Chapter 3: Students

-1-

When a high school football coach takes a job, the first noun used is "team," and the first verb he or she uses is "build." Oh sure, winning is paramount and winning is the driving force of every coach's program for if they don't win, they won't be around for very long. No, you can't make chicken salad out of chicken poop, but as long as there's poop produced, there's a chicken around with the potential to become chicken salad. Building a winning football program comes from having a good plan, selling it to the team, preparing as a team and executing as a team—none of which can happen without the communication I refer to as teaching. Once the team concept is successfully built, it becomes the informal structure for every player from the first time they step onto the field to the last time they ever pull on the old jersey. We've all heard that success breeds success. Quality management books and speakers commonly use football teams as good examples for businesses to emulate because every position is essential to the overall success of the team even though some positions get the spotlight while others are lost in obscurity.

James E. Billman

In the last chapter, I wrote that high schools can't really be considered to be businesses primarily because of their focus on the product, but if the high school would build a team in the same manner that a successful coach builds the football team the results would raise that proverbial bar to heights presently unknown. There are three reasons why this isn't done at present.

The first reason is one that will be very difficult to overcome because there is too much staff turnover in schools. Many teachers want to climb the corporate ladder, change locations for betterment or simply leave teaching for prevalent greener pastures. Teachers neither share a common professional and/or personal philosophy, nor are the results of their efforts as outwardly measurable as a football coach's. Coach knows that his job depends on success. The successful football coach really builds two teams: 1) the team that plays the game and 2) the team of assistant coaches and subordinates who support him and the program in general. The football coach will select his assistants from his personal list of criteria and place the applicants as they will fit; plus he can hire and fire pretty much as he chooses. In selecting teachers, this luxury is present only in certain fields. For instance, advertise for an elementary teacher and there will be applicants galore; advertise for a middle school position and there will be fewer applicants; advertise for a high school biology teacher and there will be fewer yet; and advertise for a high school physics teacher and there *may* be an applicant. It's difficult to put a team together if the pool of applicants isn't large for every position—a true statement in many walks of life. If there's only one player trying out for quarterback and he happens to be 4' 11" and 240 pounds there are serious concerns about how good the passing game will be. In science, if there is no physics program, how many future engineers, scientists and people in technical professions, including the medical field, will that school produce? How sad this is.

The second reason might sound like the opposite of the first. Too many teachers/coaches are concerned only with the success of the one or two arenas they're involved with. It's very difficult to be otherwise because of time demands not only in what each teacher does but what it involves to support everything else. Sometimes that support has to come in spirit, but it has to be there. It goes a long way when a teacher can take an extra step to compliment a student or other teacher for their accomplishment(s). We all know this. Actually, the football coach is often a prime example of putting his team first and the school team a distant second.

There are good and bad examples. A coach in a small school sharing a limited number of athletes in seasonally overlapping sports such as basketball and wrestling should understand that school teamwork goes a long way toward keeping harmony. In this case, because of different demands on the body, an athlete can't simultaneously compete in both. Yes, there are wrestlers that could have made good basketball players and vice versa, but the wise wrestling and basketball coaches are careful to sell their program without being disparaging toward the other coach's program. The same situation applies to the sharing of facilities between the boys' and the girls' basketball teams. If the girls' coach sees only her goals and indirectly competes with the boys' team she fails to reap the strength gleaned by mutual support of her cohorts and diminishes the success that she could have established in building a truly strong program. In a personally memorable experience exemplifying excellence, I overheard a junior high football coach asking each athlete as they left the locker room whether or not they had their homework to take home. Some students were asked specific questions about their homework showing that the coach wasn't satisfied with a simple "yes" but was actually concerned about his players' academic success.

    Thirdly, schools aren't placing the right emphasis on their products. At the present time, for some incomprehensible reason, success to a high school is measured in the percentage of graduates it produces way more than it is concerned about the quality of the graduate. This is in stark contrast to what a business entity purports to do; "Quality is job one" as Ford Motors once told us. There are a bunch of reasons why quality is important, but the foremost one in my mind is that quality will breed quantity. Again, by making school an earned privilege for the student, the reward matches the accomplishment. In other words, if the student can, he or she will. The graduation rate should be 100% discounting very few exceptions such as family emergencies, illnesses, etc. for the simple reason that if students aren't going to graduate, then they wouldn't be enrolled because they haven't "earned the privilege" to be there. When this is done, a high school diploma will mean something, and I'm pleased to see that this is gradually being done, albeit to a disappointing set of minimum standards. My thinking on this is not elitist or exclusionary; but offers a straightforward, honest opportunity for all students to achieve to their level of competency. (Remember the Peter Principle where the author contended that people achieved to one level beyond their competency? Well, this isn't the same thing.)

I started the chapter on students with this discussion because I wanted to make the point that if we do things correctly, students matriculated into schools can be gradually and totally transformed into quality products capable of representing themselves globally. Returning to the example of the football coach, a good coach can build a successful program virtually anywhere he goes and the examples abound, particularly in high school football. Coaches that do their job correctly become successful and the epitome of this truth is seen many times over in the success enjoyed by coaches in high school sports across the nation. To a person, they communicate a good game plan, they sell it, they practice it, they live it, they play it and they win by it. And the student-athletes enjoy the accolades of winning, gain the self-confidence resulting from hard work and experience success, but they also know that they were the instruments, the raw material that the coach turned into a quality product. They became chicken salad.

-2-

No discussion of students should begin or end without a disclaimer that students, like teachers and like people in every walk of life, run a gamut, a spectrum of sorts, from one extreme to the other. I have seen and enjoyed many students in my classes that taught me much more than I taught them; I am truly grateful for having earned the privilege to have communicated with them. It was my good fortune to have one or two students each year that could seemingly handle insurmountable work loads and excel in everything that they attempted. I've seen valedictorians of their class that were accomplished athletes and musicians while impeccably honorable in every possible ethical principle. To have participated in their success has been my greatest educational reward.

I've seen remarkable, high caliber individuals who didn't have the high percentile scores on standardized exams achieve and surpass their goals. I've been blessed to know students that bring a personality, a winning attitude and generous spirit who exude an aura so bright that any thought of failure is automatically precluded before it's formed. I've seen students overcome handicaps, both physical and emotional, that were used as impetuses rather than excuses to fuel amazing attainment.

I've taken joy from knowing average students as those so-called "contributors to society" that schools point their nebulous mission statements toward. Students who have not so much as played the game but did what was expected of them both by the school and in the classroom. They achieved in accordance with their school's mission statement and have…*become successful, productive, contributing citizens.* I count myself honored to have known them and count them as friends.

There was a period toward the end of my first teaching stint (twelve years) when each morning before the start of school I harbored (by their choice) a group of five students who were quite susceptible to being maligned, even bullied, by other students. I write a lot about the precocious students that go beyond expectations and the need for the school to provide the opportunity for gifted students to soar. However, this particular

Reform School

group of young men wouldn't have been in my utopian high school, but would have taken an alternate career pathway earlier in their lives before having become juniors and seniors in high school. Nevertheless, each morning we had a good time discussing sports and whatever was on our minds and no one had to take a jab to the solar plexus just for being who they were. Yes, there were times when one or the other of them told me that so-and-so had already punched him that day but they always included the directive, "Don't say anything because he'll just punch me harder next time."

  What was there that I could give these guys beyond a safe haven for twenty minutes each morning? One idea that came to me was that I could give them a personal endorsement so I told them that if they ever needed a reference to let me know. If I could help them get a job, tell me to whom I should talk or could write. I carried the thought over to my other classes and began to make it a point to individually tell each student who I thought deserving that "If you ever need a reference…" That was how I would show appreciation to those students who worked hard with the gifts with which they were endowed, and by writing recommendations, I got pretty good at it. I learned to do some things, such as mirror the criteria of the scholarship or job description; and I learned to not do other things, such as telling the selection committee what they should do. I spent a lot of time writing recommendations over my last ten years in education, and I can't recount any time better spent. It was payback for things done well, things like good attendance, good attitude and good anything in spite of extraneous circumstances. Actually, I didn't do anything but recognize and endorse in writing the qualities already present in these kids—they laid the groundwork and seized the opportunity.

And there is that other segment of the school population to which the term student can only be applied loosely. They come because they have to and they do only what they have to. We all know them. We see them in church with earphones, walking defiantly abreast in the mall and on the street. We avoid them as much as we can in public, but the law says they must be educated; therefore, they are in the schools existing solely as static to the communication of learning. The one good thing they do is help keep the building warm in the winter. The law says that everybody has a right to an education, but I say nobody has a right to keep someone else from an education.

My church tells its members that the age of reason (sic) is seven years old and children who have reached that chronological age know right from wrong. I'm sure there are exceptions even in the eyes of the church, but it's reasonable to expect kids old enough to be in the second grade to know the rules or suffer the consequences. The Jewish boy at age thirteen and the Jewish girl at age twelve become a bar mitzvah with or without ceremony because it is at that time when the Commandments holding them individually accountable go into effect. It follows in my mind that by the time students are old enough to be in high school, they are certainly old enough to be held accountable—if and only if we expect that of them. Not only do religion and faith speak to accountability, but so has history. Historically there have been a lot of mistakes and I'm not suggesting extremes such as a return to the times when an eight year old boy went to work in the coal mines by any means.

Reform School

I do tend to agree, to paraphrase the saying, that if a person is old enough to commit the crime, then he or she should do the time. I speak for accountability and responsibility for everyone capable of those qualities.

Allow some examples so I can further expound my contentions on accountability and responsibility. All examples involved high school students.

Example1: The school principal and her cohorts have worked to establish a set of rules that speak to student decorum in passing to and from classes throughout the day. They have put the expectations in writing in the student agenda booklet of which every student has a copy and is expected to adhere. Student 1 pushes the limit by being loud, boisterous and generally obstinate just to see what he can get away with. Without warning, a teacher sends the individual in violation to the principal's office whereupon the student is told to leave; he is done at that school. A school staff member escorts the student to his locker to gather his belongings, and if the student doesn't have a way home a police officer is summoned to take him.

Example 2: A classroom teacher asks her students to take out their calculators and follow her through the sample calculation. Student 2 sits in her seat and makes no indication that she has any intention of doing what she has been instructed. The teacher looks at the disobedient student, repeats the instructions in case she wasn't heard clearly the first time, and when the student still doesn't respond, she is sent to the principal's office whereupon the student is told to leave; she is done at that school and the procedure outlined in Example 1 is followed.

Example 3: A star athlete turns in a homework assignment that is copied from another student. Upon questioning by the teacher after school, during the time the athlete should be at practice, both students offer contradicting stories. The athlete claims the other student was the one who copied, and the other student says the athlete took his paper away from him so he could copy it. The teacher has both students re-do the homework assignment in her presence and easily determines who the cheater is. The consequence is the same as above—the cheater is no longer a student at the school.

Unrealistic? Too harsh? You say there would be no one left in the school by the end of the term? Read on.

The student in Example 1 tries to enroll at another school across town, but his record precedes him and is told that the rules are the same everywhere. Policy requires the student to wait one full year and then he can apply for admittance and, if his application is approved, would begin at the commencement of the next term after one full year. In the meantime, any civil violation in which the former student would be found guilty would preclude his application from being considered. And it would be the same thing for students 2 and 3. School is an earned privilege for the students and in each example students did not show that they were of the mind required to be in class.

Yes, there would be serious objections to a system that would expel students for the infractions listed. The primary argument would be that the punishment is far greater than the crime. "Why me," everybody pushes and shoves and talks too loudly in the hall, everybody has a bad day in class now and then, and everybody cheats at one time or another. I agree in principle but everybody doesn't do these things. The severity of the punishment in these cases sets the precedent and becomes a strong deterrent against infractions that are presently common. School is a place for serious business. Recall too, that the premise for my argument is that students earn the privilege to attend high school. Example #1 wouldn't even be in that school with a belligerent attitude. Example #2 might be having a bad day but she sure as heck would not broadcast it and risk losing what she has earned over something so trivial because, by now, she understands that the onus to comply is on her. Example #3 could happen, but who'd be crazy enough to throw it all away over a copied paper as there would have been an honor code, written or unwritten, in place long before the time a student got into a high school that was an "earned privilege."

Once the transition was made and the rules the same throughout the land, our schools would have the near-perfect graduation rates accomplished by students who are truly prepared to function globally. America would no longer produce students who rank 23rd in the world in mathematics ability and 17th in science. Students would have problem-solving skills, have critical thinking skills, could read for content and express their thoughts through the written word. They could do these things because they were held accountable for their actions from an early time in life and were held to a set of high standards rather than the minimum standards that exist today. Earning a high school diploma would truly be an accomplishment, and as I discuss later, would carry certain rewards. It was once that way in America and it is that way today in a lot of other places in the world—places that are no longer trying to catch up to us, but have passed us. Shift happens and it's time to make that shift

James E. Billman

change its directional goal.

-3-

I still have a lot of explaining to do in suggesting such a radical change in our schools. Perhaps a good way to do this is to move to the frequently asked questions portion of the book.

Question: *Your cockamamie notion of expelling students is in direct contrast to what you claim to be a need for accountability. What's the matter with you? How can students be taught accountability when you suggest that schools be unaccountable to keeping students in school? What happens to the kids you'd kick out of school? What a dipstick you are.- DAK, Seattle*

Answer: I refer you back to my statement that everyone has a right to education but no one has a right to deny education to someone else, which may sound like a contrasting comment also. I am not proposing kicking kids out of school, but placing them in educational programs where they can meet with success doing things that interest them. From my examples, what made the boy belligerent, the girl uncooperative and the athlete cheat? The answer isn't the success these people have met with their present curriculum, but the answer is to put them in a program that is suited to their needs where they do not need to act out negatively. No, the students kicked out of one school would then go through an intensive evaluation and subsequent placement process into a technical or trade school more suited to their aptitude and interest. If the student should continue to be a problem at a different level and gets removed again, then yes, they become Mom's and/or Dad's problem. What I'm for in the classroom is for students to be challenged, not bored; for achievement, not accommodation; and for rigor, not rigor mortis. Once the change has been affected, I doubt that my three examples would even apply because these problems would have been addressed and eliminated prior to high school.

Question: *You're proposing quite a change to an American institution that has been in place for a long time. Many people in education will not like it. Would you please explain how you would do this without saying that "shift happens"? –JJ, Omaha*

Answer: We all talk about change, but it scares the bejabbers out of those most affected by it. It will take a true paradigm shift (Is that better, JJ?) that will no doubt have some major reverberations throughout all of education. Primarily, my notion is one coming from a combination of experience and listening to the public outcry pleading for change in something that is not working. I feel that getting your toes stepped on is sometimes worth it if it is for the greater good. Actually, I'm not so sure that getting this educational system turned around and headed into the right direction isn't imminent to the survival of our country—that's how serious I view the present dilemma. As far as specifically explaining the process, I am going to defer until the final chapter when I can outline the steps in detail.

Question: *I've been in and around education for a long time, too. Knowing how slow the wheels move in a bureaucracy I can't seem to get a realistic picture of the implementation process. How can this be done? – KLS, Wichita Falls*

Answer: First there needs to be consensus that a major overhaul is needed. I'm not pompous enough to think that my idea will be accepted in its entirety or that I have all of the answers. But later in the book when I lay out my perception of global education, you will see that I suggest using think tanks and brainstorming that, although American in origin, have been used to better advantage elsewhere in the world, particularly in wresting industry away from us. It should start in homes where parents are dissatisfied, in faculty meetings where fortitudinous teachers stand up and defiantly take a stand, in the classrooms where disgruntled students recognize and insist on their right to an education, in school board meetings, in restaurants, club meetings and with a truly concerned editorial media. These singular activities then come together not so much with a plan as with a common voice that there must be a change for the better. In short, it has begun; it's called public outcry and the next step is unification. People close to education, who aren't disillusioning themselves, realize that if we "keep on keeping on" the slide downhill gets faster and faster.

Question: *Doesn't the governing body decide what happens in education? – JJJ, Salt Lake City.*

Answer with another question: Who is the governing body in a democracy?

Question: *How would you structure all this beneficially? JEB – Kentucky*

A long answer with a few questions: I'm glad I asked that; I've wanted to explain my idea to get kids involved at an early age. Having sat in teacher meetings, seminars, workshops and outhouses with K-12 teachers, I have noticed a wide disparity of knowledge. In pursuing a Master's degree, one of my classes was a practicum where I worked as a graduate assistant in a

Reform School

general science class for elementary teachers. These teachers approached this class with a trepidation that I could hardly believe—they were afraid of science and openly admitted that they didn't know anything about it. In other instances at so many workshops that required a calculation or two, no matter how basic, I'd hear "You're the math person, you do it for us." Who and what is this "math person?" I've heard principals defer any reference to working an equation or speaking knowingly about a statistic. C'mon, we're all math people and we need to get over it. I saw a saying once that went something like this: "The odd thing about the man who says 'I can' and the man who says 'I can't' is that they are both right." I am not convinced that we are teaching ourselves and our progeny to focus their energy toward a positive goal.

    High school teachers are less the generalist and more the specialist but it's the other way around in the lower grades, which smacks of an upside down system. Why not put teachers who are experts in subject matter areas in the lower grades and challenge them to instill in their students the benchmarks of education that we now hold out for high school students? Aren't we told that young children can learn foreign languages quite easily, or at least comparatively easier than adults? No, I'm not proposing a qualitative chemistry course for fourth graders, but at the same time, I don't know of anyone taking the course in high school either beyond small little pockets here and there. I've had chemistry classes in which my students were incapable of lighting and adjusting a Bunsen burner without my direct supervision. Long story short, put the subject matter experts in the lower grades, but still allow recesses and the necessary physical activities commensurate with their physically developmental age. Teach children to be orderly and disciplined and because this is our expectation of them, it will happen. Think about it.

And a final comment in thinking about all the axons and dendrites to and from the brain. It would seem diligent to either impact or extract all the information possible early in one's school life rather than wait five to eight years when more tangles exist. Maybe learning is like combing your hair after washing it—it's a lot easier if you comb it right away than to wait an hour or so.

-4-

In the introduction to this book I mentioned my qualifications to expound on education. One of them was my span of three so-called generations: my own school days, those students in my early days as a teacher, and more recently, the children of students that I had in my early days. For virtually all career teachers, the arena of their experience and knowledge widens even further because teachers work together, young and old, sharing their experiences informally. And moreover, non-teachers talk to teachers about their school experiences. I am far from unique with my accumulated knowledge of education but well accorded with my fellow educators when I speak for reform.

The *Eighth Grade Kansas Graduation Exam of 1895* has been making the rounds for a while, having been on the internet with the intention of making us think about how far education has deteriorated since the "good old days." It had sections on Grammar (one hour), Arithmetic (75 minutes), U.S. History (45

Reform School

minutes), Orthography (one hour), and Geography (one hour). Obviously dated by both language and dimensional units, the questions could quite easily be paraphrased to the vernacular and would present a substantial challenge for students today. It's interesting to note that at this time there was also a Normal School test that teachers-in-training had to take that was not unlike the Eighth Grade Test. I suppose the professors that graded these exams were equally critical of the deterioration in future teachers' ability from one generation to the next.

I once made a statement to the effect that the high school education of the 1950's and 1960's produced a person with a better general knowledge than a college education does in this century. What I said was perhaps controversial but was definitely not profound for there is no way of determining the accuracy because of the transcendence of time. People that graduated in 1960 have the benefit of all the time between 1942 and the present, whereas the college graduate of this year was probably born in the late 1980's. The proverbial School of Hard Knocks that gives the class of '60 a fifty year advantage learning life's experiences probably supplants a four year college education quite readily. Rather typically, I engaged my mouth before my brain; it's often been quite easy to do. However, most of us older people do agree that education has slipped over the years. So, what's really happened over these three generations that I lay claim to knowing something about? What has affected this apparent change in students between then and now?

My grandmother and grandfather with whom my mother and I lived while my father was in the army during World War II had parents who lived through the Civil War. Some of my

James E. Billman

earliest memories include the taste of molasses cookies made because of the sugar rationing. My grandparents and parents lived through the Great Depression, which was an experience that marked their behavior throughout. As a child I remember little scraps of food that my grandmother had wrapped and saved for later. Likewise, a week's trash rarely filled more than a paper sack. I also recall pieces of wood too small for anything practical stacked along the wall of the garage and a can of bent nails in the basement waiting to be straightened and re-used that my father saved—each the result of the lasting impression of those times.

My maternal grandfather was a railway postal clerk and sorted mail in a train car. I recently visited a train museum and mentioned this fact to the tour guide and she had no recollection of this ever having been a job. Nevertheless, he rode back and forth from Burlington to Galesburg to Peoria to Chicago for almost thirty years. As far as postal jobs went, his was one of the more prestigious positions; it was said that a postal clerk had to know the location of 10,000 post offices in his area in order to put the correct envelopes in the correct pigeon holes and then into mailbags, all done prior to the instigation of Zip Codes. If I had planned for this to be my career when I was in school it would have been difficult to find a job because the number of railway postal clerks started to decline after World War II, and the very last car was taken out of circulation in 1977 when they were replaced by the short-lived U.S. Mail buses.

My mother and father also lived through the Great Depression; each affected independently but lastingly. My father-in-law, of which I have written previously, was the same age as my father but lived in the Midwest on an 80-some acre farm with an impossible mortgage on it. My mother-in-law was in England amid that country's problems as she waited with her countrymen for the next aggressive onslaught from the Nazi Luftwaffe.

    My father quit school after the seventh grade to work in a Pennsylvania shoe factory where most of the people in the town also worked. He was a wood saver and built our "new" garage out of reclaimed lumber using crossbeams from old telephone poles as the wall studs. He had previously taken apart an old building and used boards from the sub-floor for sheathing on both the walls and roof while the old floor joists became the new rafters. He held it all together with the bent nails that had been straightened against a piece of iron that had once been part of a railroad track. The plate glass window from the front of the old building became a picture window in our house and the steel beam above the old window made a perfect header for his garage door.

    As a child, I watched my father and those like him rejoin their families when they came home from the war, but their determination didn't register with me at the time. I hadn't known the depression; I hardly knew of it until assigned to read *The Grapes of Wrath* in college. I did see that my father's hard work and frugality allowed us to move out of an apartment and into an old house that eventually became a nicely remodeled home. If anything, my generation learned that hard work paid off.

    My wife and I bought an older house not much more than a year after I came home from Vietnam. We started out a move ahead of our parents, but we had the lessons of hard work instilled in us as children. Our daughters, not that they didn't struggle to make ends meet, made a quantum leap as one had a new house built to specification and the other started her married life in a newer home in a San Diego suburb appraised at over $400,000. Without a memory of the Great Depression and its effects, each following generation was given more choices, the best one of them being the opportunity for educational attainment. For all of us, however, accomplishments were the result of a formal education that was earned, not given. We all paid our own way although the lifestyles around us were forever changing.

I'm not so sure that this work ethic over the generations has been consistent in our public schools. Not that hard work has been eschewed since then, but I think innovation and patience have been the unfortunate trade-off for acquisition. In America, today's society finds things to be readily available; people don't carry the haunting memories of depressions and/or of major wars. Today, many individuals look laterally and see what other people are doing and what they have acquired. I think much of the American ideal has been lost to complacency and, of course, it carried over into the classrooms. I saw little innovation or patience in my last five years of teaching.

To students, class work is too slow in a technically-induced dynamic world. Math has become something that can be left for someone else to do. Science is often met with a "so what's that supposed to mean to me" lackadaisical attitude. Computers can check their spelling (orthography), grammar and provide information on virtually any subject so the processes of laboring over word-selection, syntax and basic rules of language aren't of concern. History can be seen by watching movies, and many students have been told that it is tainted in their history books. Students are different today and often act like impertinent smart-alecky dunderheads to many of us because the interests and experiences of this generation are not shared with a past generation.

I do not make a plea of the need for schools to keep up with today's technology simply because, no matter how much money is poured into the technological coffers of a school, it can't be done. Believe me, a school can spend its (our) money so much more wisely than trying to keep up with technology. I recall a member of the Advisory Board at the community college telling us not to worry about our students having the latest and greatest equipment to train on because every major company in industry has their own machines, processes and methods that were at least a generation beyond our school's newest equipment. He explained that he only wanted our school to supply his company with graduates that knew the basics of the job for which they were training and with that alone, they could easily matriculate into the positions within his organization. Knowing this from my days at the community college, it was excruciatingly painful to witness the lack of concern in high school students over how fundamental natural laws and principles drove the apparatus of today's technology. I dubbed today's apathetic students as the "who cares, as long as it works" generation.

This is a difficult concept to grasp; we see the results of change but we haven't necessarily changed ourselves. School-age kids play with video games, see movies on telephones, and incessantly watch all sorts of things via computer enhancements without understanding the underlying principles, both scientific and economic, that drive the mechanisms. Most students know what a pixel is but can't grasp the significance of the cathode ray tube (CRT) or explain the electromagnetic spectrum. Worse yet, they don't seem to care. They can't light a Bunsen burner but in many places can legally drive a car traveling one hundred feet per second while simultaneously eating a foot-long sandwich, talking on a cell phone and fixing their makeup. The generation gap and the stagnation that has inhibited global thinking are front and center in addressing the perceived decline of the American student. All of us see the changes in our world and the changes make their needs different today than education, which has not changed, perceives them to be. Perhaps many of the educational specialists see apathy when the problem is really dissociation; an area where the experts could focus their efforts as they reform schools.

-5-

I often mention the existence of a major difference over the three generations of education in which I've been involved. The demographics tell us that students in today's high schools do not achieve as well as students one and two generations ago. The demographics also tell us that former third world countries have attained educational achievement levels beyond us–way beyond us. China's school-age students go to school for twice as many hours as American children. China's eighth grade students have already had biology, chemistry and physics. I had the privilege to have had a Chinese exchange student in both my Talented and Gifted and Physics classes who confirmed this. Conversely, my ninth grade students were no more ready for their study of biology than they were to explain surgical procedures to medical students.

I have also made reference to my belief that students are a constant, and although the word "manipulative" may be too strong, students are certainly pliable. The good football coach molds his team by offering an end that is worth the means, yet high school test scores plummet because society has distanced itself and left formal education solely in the hands of the school. The field of education takes the wrong fork in the road and decides to improve what they have been doing rather than looking outwardly for what else they might do to serve the needs of the modern-day student, and thereby fails miserably. The result is that they have bought into a program that says minimum standards are acceptable standards, and American students annually fall farther behind in core subjects. This is just fine with the students because they don't know any different or recognize what it means. Many students haven't been 60 miles away from where they were born; they haven't experienced a depression, they aren't old enough to understand inflation and they live in a disposable society. What do they know about global issues when many of the places where they live have allowed the need to go global pass them by? No, don't see the K-12 students so much as the perpetrators of decline, but see them more as the victims.

Students aren't beans in a can any more than they are automobiles coming off the assembly line but they are still corporately pliable. The function of a school is to make use of this fact as we use communication, informally and formally, to shape them into globally functional members of society. Yes, students are different; classrooms are representative of 27 different personalities that spread across a spectrum ranging from poverty to opulence, from snake-kissing evangelists to devout atheists and from philanthropists to "What, me worry?" Alfred E. Neuman© types.

    Here's an example from my experiences that I would use on students. "Okay people; let's have a vote on whether to have a test on Thursday or Friday. If we have it on Thursday, there won't be time for a review, but most of you have done really well on the work in this chapter. There's also a big game Friday that will be on your minds; those infidels from Bumtown will be here. If we wait until Friday, that's fine with me as it will give me all weekend to get them graded."

    Not noticeably catching the innuendos and propaganda I was using, they'd vote for Thursday and think that I was pretty democratic in the way I ran my classroom. And if it wasn't going my way I might ask if anyone in the class already had a test scheduled for Friday. And if I still didn't sense the vote going my way, I'd offer a carrot by referring to reviewing the test on Friday "while it's still fresh in your mind." I wanted the test to be on Thursday yet had not said anything negative about having the test on Friday.

    Another observation about students: I would use the pliability of students by having them write about themselves under the ploy of allowing me to "get to know them," which is what I wanted to do, but I would also learn about their family's belief systems and ideologies. I'd save their papers and use them to build the informal relationship that I thought was so important

Reform School

for formal communication (learning). I would also read them prior to parent-teacher conferences to not only gain some insight on why the student's performance was what it was as well as to enhance my ability to communicate with the parent. I don't like to think that I used this information to tell the parents what they wanted to hear about their child, but it did help me to be tactful in the manner in which we would have our discussion.

Speaking of conferences, I can't help but throw in a little sidebar in order to grouse about all those other things the administration would have teachers do because plain and simple, they didn't trust teachers to effectively do things on their own. "Be sure to save your tests. Have writing samples available. Show parents samples of their child's work. Have a grade printout to give them. Contact every parent at least a week prior and invite them to the conference. Give each parent a scheduled time to come, fill out the following schedule and bring it to the office, both before the conference and after the conference." Yada, yada.

Allow me to put all this together. Axiomatically, we all know that: 1.We are initially *who* we are, *where* we are, and *what* we are by pure chance mainly because we haven't unraveled a grander scheme. The fourth "w", *why*, however, has nothing to do with the other three. 2. *What* we do with *who* we are and *where* we are is the free will ascribed to our species; we have choices. 3. Our environment or surroundings, plays a defining role that exerts a powerful influence that can be both positive and negative on our lives; hence, the accountability of our choices and the ensuing responsibility for them. 4. We know best what we have experienced, which makes us products of our environment, however narrow or broad it might be.

I have contended that once a child has reached the age of reason, which in my mind ranges from age five to definitely no more than eight, each is responsible for his/her own actions and should be held accountable. I've read accounts of family life chronicled in books where an older sibling of age five was expected to take care of the younger ones while everyone else worked in the fields. Discussions abound concerning how focused mentalities are brought about in children—how a parent, guardian, teacher or anyone in charge affects optimum behavior that promotes responsibility and accountability involving leadership, knowledge, consistency and a whole battery of admirable attributes that work. If there was a right way, we would all do it. In my experiences and experiences of many in my age range, force was an option; whatever befell us at school for our misdeeds would befall us with twice the impact at home. As a parent, the best way for my wife and me to "influence" our children's behavior was with a face-to-face no-nonsense lecture about how one person's behavior reflected on the entire family. We made it important to have our children know that making favorable impressions on others was important, so do not do things that disgrace us. This was a rather Eastern psychology that we learned from our friends that, in turn, taught our children early in life that they were not the center of the universe. I remember telling my children at least ten million times about the importance of "all the horses in the team have to pull in the same direction" to get the job done correctly and honorably. It worked pretty well for my wife and me with our children both at home and throughout their school days because today our children tell us how they are doing the same things with their children.

To my way of thinking, at age 5 a child goes to school with certain expectations explained to them. If they can't do it, they are sent home. Certain expectations are not the problem of the school or the teacher if they cannot do what is expected of them for school is always an earned privilege. Of course schools must clearly define their expectations and keep them within reason for each group. It would be pretty tough to expel a little boy or girl who couldn't follow the rules based on one episode, so there must be a period of time when the offending student is allowed to become acclimated or socialized; a time to understand that "this is how we do it around here." With a little practice, children who have been told simply and effectively the consequences for not following the rules should be able to adapt to them. I sincerely believe that starting early in having expectations and holding a child responsible for his or her actions goes a long way for attaining later success in life's pursuits.

I also think that the role of parents and teachers has to be played with skill. Parenting, as teaching, is an ongoing art form that carries its own very serious responsibility; responsibility that can't be passed on if it doesn't exist in the first place. When I recall the three young mothers in my freshman biology class, I can't map a successful course for their children because their mom's are not much more than children themselves. I do know good things can happen and they certainly have in cases such as these in the past, and I hope there are enough positive influences for these three mothers and their babies. But the odds of it happening just aren't there.

No matter what the child's upbringing may involve,

whether it ranges from none to too much, I cannot look at poor classroom behavior on the part of a student and think "oh, it's not their fault, the poor little dears." That's bullcrap. If a student couldn't manage himself or herself by the time they got to the classes I taught, I held them totally responsible—not their previous teachers, not their peers, not their parents, not the administration or that culprit of culprits, their hormones. Optimally there needs to have been a modicum of discipline from home early in life and a consistency from teachers and administrators throughout their trek through school. With students having been given expectations with real consequences, schools could become centers of real academic achievement more than capable of competing on a global scale.

-6-

No discussion of students is complete without mentioning what I intone to be a real problem; a problem that takes the time, the space and the individual into account. Namely, at what point does a student become disenchanted, turned off if you will, in school? Any actual point would be similar to determining the age of reason in having not as much to do with a physiological age as with one's level of maturity. It wouldn't be fair to say that a person unequivocally reaches the age of reason at age seven if he is a Roman Catholic or at age 12 if she's Jewish and at age 13 if he's Jewish. There has to be a place, not a point but a sliding scale or range in time where a large number of students lose interest because most of them reach that place in their lives where school holds little or no interest for them. Not that all students do lose interest and not that all interest is totally lost as much

Reform School

as it is done in degrees or percentages; an "I don't understand math, but I like geography" type of thing. Define it however you'd like, but there's a series of transitions where something that started as a spark, became a flame and now sets on the grate as a cold ash. Little kids love school. They come home from school and "play" school with their siblings or dolls. It seems that so many questions about learning habits could be answered if we knew about the events and circumstances that bring about this loss of interest; the extinguishing of the flame. We see the disenchantment—it's visible, but we miss the timing and the treatment. We also know that it will affect every student to some degree or another, which makes it so important to communicate with each child and to be a presence in his or her life.

    My school boy experiences of becoming disinterested came when I got distracted and found other things, like girls and the dynamics of the present moment to dampen my flame for things academic. I remember not being able to focus on World History in spite of having an excellent teacher. I remember sitting in English class and shooting a scrap of paper across the top of my desk engrossed in an imaginary golf game. I remember going from being distracted to being a distraction in Latin. By the time I went into the Army, specifically Officer Candidate School, I could make myself invisible so I wouldn't get singled out to answer a question that I neither heard nor could have answered if I had been paying enough attention to hear it. I became a teacher in order to help others get what I couldn't give myself as a student—I felt guilty for having been such a poor student, and I wanted to help others not make the same mistakes I had.

    My last teaching job was marked with inconsistency

James E. Billman

because I was the stranger to the area and brought expectations from my past job like "students should be in their seats, be quiet and ready for class by the time the bell rings." My "new" school gave teachers duties (imagine that) outside of the classroom, and I would observe a majority of students taking nothing home on a daily basis. A full 85% of them took no books with them as they got on the school bus or scurried to their cars. At first, until students found out that I read every word on every page of homework, I got some real pieces of trash handed in, if I got anything at all. Most of the teachers and administrators and guidance counselors and custodial staff in this high school blamed the middle school for the study habits and the behavior of the students when they first came into our school. I wonder who the middle school teachers blamed. I wonder who the elementary teachers blamed. I wonder who the parents blamed. Parents would say to me, "I just can't seem to make him mind." Well Mom and Dad (if you're there), love your kid enough to teach them responsibility and accountability. And guess what, giving in to them when they're young is asking for a lot of trouble when they get older. Communicate!

My infamous biology class supposedly consisted of students who would take one of the harder causeways to their diploma. They were what the school called Honors Program students but, as ninth graders, had not yet earned any honors, but had informed the counselors that they were college-bound. High school biology was not for this group of freshmen, but that's the way it was done (Kindly recall that this is the school that did not offer physics because not enough students signed up for it.) The biology textbook weighed considerably more than eight pounds, had over a thousand pages and this particular edition had been in circulation for seven years in this school. Each of the 53 chapters consisted of two to four lessons that were conveniently arranged into 45 minute class sessions. There were laboratory exercises, workbooks and exams. In a typical chapter of three daily lessons there were generally 30-45 definitions. Our school was on a block schedule and each class period was ninety minutes. The classroom had sixteen chairs at eight tables, one desk-seat molded together and lab stools for the remaining eleven students. Add to this frenzy a teacher who had a biology emphasis from a teacher's college, but had taught biology only once in his lifetime—precisely forty years ago. Remember how I mentioned that we teachers blamed the middle schools for the lack of discipline and motivation in our students? I was with the supposed *crème de la crème* of the ninth grade that included only six boys, the three mothers mentioned before and fourteen beauty queens. Every one of the beauty queens and definitely all of the mothers had to go to the restroom each day, even though it was frowned upon by the administration for teachers to let them go unless it was an emergency (one of those very unenforceable rules). Further, three of the six boys had a combined grade at the end of the term that didn't add up to 100. In all fairness to those five or six who tried to do well in the class, the rest probably never read one lesson in the book from start to finish. As a teacher, I felt that I was a miserable failure because I did not know what to do; I never did have their attention on anything academic. I used worksheets and tested about every third day over a chapter. I picked only the easier, more interesting chapters (I let them vote.), went to the other teachers in the school who were also

James E. Billman

teaching biology whose best advice was "fail them if they don't do anything. Don't worry about it." I did worry about it. In the end, I think six students did fail, and I dashed the dreams of being a straight-A student for all but one of the rest of the class. Here was a classic case of lose-lose that ranks sadly as the worst experience of my teaching career, even worse than when the community college student felt compelled to show me his knife because I had confronted him when he had cheated on a test.

So do I blame the students for the way they act, for not reading, for cheating on homework and copying exams, for not having the self-discipline to be prepared for class? Yes, I do. Do I blame students for taking no responsibility for self and family esteem, for not being accountable for their performance and not being farsighted enough to perceive their own best interest? Yes, I do.

Here's another experiential story that takes generations to be able to tell. When I started teaching, everyone in the class would at least come to order and give me the benefit of the doubt during class time; there were more students in the class that wanted to learn than who didn't want to learn. The latter group faked it but they were no distraction to the first group. Today the non-interested learners rule and the people who would learn if the conditions were right (the "Archies") won't speak up and say "Hey, I want to know," and they consequently suffer. I could honestly say that I had one student of 81 during my last semester who would speak up for himself and maybe a dozen others whom I would call "serious students."

I shared with my classes my observation that the news coverage of the war-torn and natural disaster areas of the world

Reform School

would often air footage showing children who are elated at being able to go to school or return to their school. These kids were happy just to be able to have a school, with or without a roof whereas my students in America would whine if the room was a bit too warm for their tastes. I once talked with a few students in Vietnam who loved school and hoped their school wouldn't get bombed or destroyed. In other areas of the region, I saw ravished, blown-up schools whose students had no place to go; those kids weren't screaming and hollering in joy because there would be no school tomorrow. The American students wherever I taught were overjoyed when there was an early dismissal for something like a snowstorm. We still see kids in third world countries working with crude learning devices such as slates, where our kids show resentment if they don't have a computer at their disposal. Yeah, I blame the kids for the way they are; for their apathy, their insolence, their diffidence, their unresponsiveness and their uncooperativeness.

But at the same time, I saw the squalor and wretched lifestyles that many of the families had to endure as I traveled about in the districts where I taught. Every now and then a worthwhile seminar or teacher's meeting was offered and those that dealt with poverty gave us some insight into the loudness, the fierce pride and the "what will be will be" fatalistic attitude of many kids living in poverty. It wrenched my heart when, by the third week of the term, I recognized students as much by their only tee shirt as by their face, but it irked me to watch them act out against the establishment rather than seeing the opportunity that school offered as a vehicle to escape their impoverishment. The obtrusive students as well as the diffident students in this group no doubt got these attitudes from someone else, they weren't inborn. Please don't construe what I'm arguing to think that I believe poverty is an illness or anathema we can simply avoid. There's an entire range of conditions, circumstances and incidences that have truly forced people to be without. No, I understand poverty—fully.

Do I blame the parents who run the gamut from indifference to being over-protective? Yes I do, but I can't tell them how to do it. There are no formulas or equations, only that bunch of quality terms listed earlier in the chapter. Parenting is a social science, which is so much harder than a natural science to understand. I blame parents who give up, who acquiesce to their children and who don't hold them to standards. Although I believe in unconditional love for one's child, I am not a subscriber to "My child, right or wrong."

I also blame the community, the state, and the nation for fostering the stagnation that caused so many places to miss out on the global revolution. It appalls me to hear a stumping politician promise to bring high-paying industrial jobs to the area because it tells me they don't understand—there are not now and will not be any high paying industrial jobs because of the global economy. My last semester in college, I worked a full-time job at the John Deere plant on the second shift. I started on the assembly line as a fill-in putting the rear right axle assembly together on tractors, *4020's* and *2010's*. I was all thumbs for the first few hours, but gradually learned the moves and by the end of the second night, I could keep up. After a week, I had time to wait for the next rear end to descend from overhead (No, I'm not trying to be punny!). The point is, given the opportunity, many people the world over could do the same thing. However at that time, in 1965, America and namely the Midwest was one of the few industrialized parts of the world and my earnings then were far more than I would earn four years later in my first teaching job. Since John Deere was unionized, there wasn't much global competition from other tractor makers and we had the facility—the prized commodities, the machines, that are no longer prized at all and won't be in the future because of availability. Yes the politician might bring industry to his or her area, but it definitely won't be as good as the workers at John Deere enjoyed forty-some years ago.

This failure to morph with the global shifts has fostered a serious carry-over to the attitudes of many students in our schools—attitudes that they have without knowing the deep-seated reason why. An attitude was fostered and passed on to them when all the coal was mined, when farm machinery replaced most farm hands, when the railroads were deemed to be no longer effective, when the steel mills closed, and industry went elsewhere. Few displaced workers would admit that the lack of foresight cost them dearly and few would admit their culpability in losing their job and being laid-off without a contingency. Because it was so hard to admit responsibility, it was easier to push blame onto someone else, and rather than learn from the event and not let it happen again, self-pity emerged. And it still hurts deeply to admit it.

Along the same line, thousands of cities across America are faced with serious and expensive infrastructure deficiencies today simply because "if it wasn't broken, it wasn't...maintained. It's the old proscriptive-prescriptive thing all over.

James E. Billman

One last comment, how many times do teachers hear "It's all about the kids" in the course of a year? Is that why I read in the newspaper about highly successful remedial mathematics courses for incoming college freshmen? Why do we even have a need to teach high school graduates remedial math unless something is wrong in their preparation program in high school? If it's all about the kids, is that why most 100-level (freshmen) college courses automatically assume to be remedial? In education-ese, "remedial" assumes no prior knowledge on the part of the student. If it's all about the kids, then why are we satisfied with minimum standards in our schools? And if it's all about the kids, why do we let them reach the age of reason without teaching them responsibility and accountability?

Reform School

Real Life Adventure #3

There had been a terrible ice storm the previous night and even though it hadn't come without warning, Mother Nature had malevolently re-arranged the sequence of events to make it worse than expected. Roads throughout the area had been salted in preparation but instead of the prognosticated ice, six hours of steady rain preceded the overnight sleet and had consequently washed the salt off the roads. The lowering temperature from the ensuing sleet froze the existing water and the compounding result left a thick, heavy coating of ice on everything from door jambs to birds' beaks. Branches had fallen on houses and roads and downed overhead lines brought the entire county to a halt as emergency crews frantically began to repair what seemed to be an insurmountable task. Thousands of homes had no electricity and some folks would have to endure without power for as long as a week. Although ice storms were fairly common to the area, this was one for the record books.

After arising to a slowly cooling house, a retired mathematics teacher looked out of his windows and announced to his wife that a large branch had fallen very close to the house and that the entire front yard was strewn with debris. This was their first winter in the area having chosen to move from the brutally cold winters of the upper Midwest to a more southerly region known for its milder winter temperatures. There had been other environmental changes along with higher temperatures: topographically, trees had replaced prairie; meteorologically, ice was more common than snow; and culturally, there was a different societal subset that reached far beyond dialect.

Since making the move when he retired, there had been occasions where both the teacher and his wife questioned the wisdom of their choice. Not only had the cost of the move far exceeded their estimates but they had failed to consider the difficulty involved in leaving their "comfort zone" to come to a place where they were not known. He was a long-time teacher and she had worked in retail, they had raised their children there and taken an active role in the community for over thirty years. By their longevity they were taken for granted and enjoyed the liberties familiarity accorded, which was not the situation in their new location for they had completely overlooked the fact that the liberties are earned, not given. That they were outsiders betrayed them in their speech, their colloquialisms and their expectations. In fact, it would be fair to say that the teacher became somewhat of a bitter old curmudgeon throughout the accommodation process. In a letter to a former colleague he wrote:

...We live in a town that can't quite define itself: it doesn't know whether it wants to hold on to tradition or hold itself out to progress, it sets stubbornly astraddle the still-present Mason-Dixon Line, and it has too many people with the same last name. Over twenty trains course through the heart of the city during all

hours on a daily basis, the main traffic thoroughfares are both too few and too restrictive for timely passage and the neighborhoods are too distinctive—several of them have deteriorated beyond restoration or repair. In sharing experiences with others, we have been told that the business owners are known for their callous behavior to folks they don't know and service people seem to specialize in extortion. I must say that I concur with the sentiment.

Earlier this summer, I asked a local lawn service to give me a quote and was told that there's usually 35 times per year that his helpers would mow and he'd do it for two thousand dollars. We do have a double lot, but $57.14 per mow seemed pretty expensive so I declined and decided to do it myself. Fact is, we've had a dry summer and I mowed the yard a total of six times all year. We had a bad ice storm last winter and a man came by when I was out in the yard picking up limbs and offered to do it for two hundred dollars. I told him that I'd do it myself and his offer immediately came down to $150. Persistent, I still said that I'd get it done by myself and then he said he'd do it for $100. Maybe I'm getting old, but it kind of made me mad to think that the man tried to screw me out of $100 when he could have done the job and still probably had a nice profit for a hundred. Back home, a person would never do business that way. It's surely different down here....

The fact that localities and areas differ throughout the country not only affect attitudes but schools as well. Local folkways and mores are fine and admirable because they speak to the preservation of heritage, but they're not so fine when they become a form of isolationism. As the protagonist from the passage above, the teacher erred in thinking that he could bring the intangibles of his former life with him, and in finding himself unable to do this, he became angry and quick to criticize. Although he did have some justifiable reasons to complain when others tried to take advantage of him, it was because he was not aware of the way it was done in this particular place. We need to be knowledgeable of the fact that we all are affected by not only who we are and what we are, but where we are and how long we have been there. It took a lot of time, a lot of retrospective thinking and a lot of help from his wife before the retired teacher realized that he had lived one of the most important lessons that need to be taught in our schools. The point is this: Schools need to teach both locally and globally if we are going to live in harmony.

Later that fall, the retired math teacher had another experience that once again involved some bad weather and his trees. It was a chilly, blustery day in late October as the teacher looked through the work wanted advertisements in the newspaper for a tree trimmer. On a page designed for trades people to place small ads, the teacher saw four of them, each professing the fact that they were, in one way or another "a cut above" their competitors. There were three very large trees in the teacher's front yard that needed some branches trimmed for they were a potential to fall on his house in a strong wind or possibly another ice storm.

With past experiences in mind, the teacher called one of the numbers listed in the advertisements and heard the recording that told him the number was no longer in service. A second call was answered and the man said he would try to come by in a "couple hours" but never did. On the third call a woman answered and upon inquiry reported that the teacher could leave his name and number and the tree trimmer would call back—"no wait, here he comes now." The teacher held for the trimmer to get to the phone and listened to the footsteps as the man slowly approached the phone. "Hullo," in a non-enthusiastic voice with no mention of the business, but with all due respect for the fellow, it was Saturday afternoon and he had no doubt worked very hard all week as tree work is quite physical.

    The teacher explained his concern and the trimmer thought he could make it over to look at the trees in question in about an hour—no promises. This particular trimmer did come, and the matter was discussed amid chin-rubbing, waving, pointing and a myriad of "hmms." There was no writing, no references to a price list, no pictures taken or any indication that any kind of a contract would be drawn. In the teacher's eyes the man was not considering the amount of work in the job as much as he was sizing up the teacher, his house and the neighborhood so he could make the ensuing estimate as high as the tree trimmer thought he could—the old poker game again. He listed all the factors that made the job peculiarly difficult: the trees were very tall, the house was precariously close, and the moon was on the rise. He didn't verbally mention that there were no power lines nearby, that the teacher's large lot posed no problem for other homes or that whatever equipment the trimmer brought would have no problem getting close to the work. He also speculated that the middle tree alone would cost $1200 if the teacher chose to "top" it rather than trim it, so trimming all three of them for $800 would be a real good deal. The trimmer proceeded to explain what branches he would cut and that his service would include cutting, hauling and cleaning for the estimated price. He could come either the very next Monday or Tuesday, depending.

Again the teacher's mind came back to the ice storm episode with the other man and in comparing the money he had earned for a day of teaching school with the offer from the tree trimmer, it seemed pretty high. No, the teacher was no haggler and he still didn't understand why a contractor in this part of the United States would always offer an exorbitant figure when first estimating a job; it was a tenuous, confrontational way to conduct business. He told the trimmer that he would have to think about the offer before making a decision as well as getting a bid from the other tree trimmer he had called—the man who never did come. The teacher would also ask his neighbor, a life-long resident of the area, what the going price might be for a job of this magnitude. (Later, in doing this the neighbor thought it was at least $300 too high.)

The teacher walked the tree trimmer to his truck as they chatted about trees. Somewhere in the conversation the teacher mentioned that he had taught for a long period of time and his subject had been high school mathematics. The tree trimmer said that his daughter was in the fourth grade and he didn't understand the crazy way they taught math anymore, nothing like it had been when he went to school. He explained to the teacher that now they were assigning letters to numbers and it troubled him that his daughter's teacher would make her do math "that they will never use again."

The teacher sensed that he should say something that might explain what was actually being taught, but he didn't want to sound offensive so he simply said that it was computer math; that the fourth graders were probably being taught how a computer does math. He also said something like "I think the number ten is represented with an "A" and they use the letters of the alphabet up to the number 15."

"Yeah, I think 'A' was 10, but why would they do that? Fifteen is fifteen and not some letter; it doesn't make sense the way they do things anymore."

The teacher responded by mentioning, "Well, we are in the computer age."

After the man had gone the teacher reflected on the conversation thinking about what he might have said but hadn't, "You better hope these kids have a chance to use their math skills in later life because if they don't, they're not giving themselves much of a chance to compete for jobs in the face of new technology. What you don't envision for the future is limited only by your imagination and has little bearing on what will actually come, so by all means, don't let your perception of what today's youth will need in the future constrain your daughter. Take part in what she's learning and if you see no reason for it, ask her math teacher to enlighten you so you can understand. While it's true that most of us don't use our accumulated math skills on a daily basis we find them quite useful in understanding the world around us and help us as functioning, informed and contributing members to a global society. Just as you don't use every tool in your tool- box on a daily basis it's nice to know those tools are there when you do need them. What your daughter learns in school becomes part of her personal toolbox and the more tools she has to face the future, the more jobs she'll be able to do throughout life and the more self-worth she will have."

The teacher also wished that the trimmer would somehow come to understand how so many parents undermine the work done by teachers in so many of their efforts at teaching, particularly at teaching skills used in a technological age. Oftentimes, even seemingly innocuous remarks made at home can damage what is being taught at school.

It had never been enough to the teacher to merely poke the external keys on electronic devices without having an understanding of the internal mathematical keys that made it happen. In actuality, he would have liked to commend that girl's teacher for her wisdom in teaching computer mathematics and helping her students understand digital coding. That kind of learning is empowering.

Later in the day, the teacher talked to his wife about how the parents who are the primary teachers in a child's life have so much more influence than any classroom teacher, and if they aren't working in concert with each other, the student, especially a young impressionable student, is likely to side with the parent's point of view. "It is devastating to think how easily parents wipe out the work of the school when they start criticizing without taking the time to ask why."

At the close of the day, the tree trimmer did not have the job and the retired teacher had put aside trimming his trees as he spent the rest of the day in a state of semi-depression because of the effect parental attitudes of negativism have on many young minds. Maybe he'd trim his trees by himself. In passing, the immortal words of Kurt Vonnegut came to him, "So it goes."

Reform School

4: Parents

-1-

Parents are the singular most important teachers that any child has. Whatever happens in school, anywhere, anytime or anyplace it is secondary to the role that a parent plays as a teacher, and it is imperative for this select group to step up, take charge and carry it through. Imagine the void created when no one with this authority is there to communicate with a child. So the first rule for any parent or person in a child's life who fills that role is: Be there! The second most important thing is: Teach! Unfortunately, there are instances when that can't be done and a heck of a lot more cases where it isn't done.

I won't offer a list of tips to good parenting mainly because I don't know any that work in all cases, and I see little or no value in ambiguous lists citing the "ten most important…". The point is that parenting is an ongoing experiment that takes place in the present—it's now, the proverbial 24/7. Sure, we can plan ahead and can self-assess but for the vast majority of times, parenting is of the moment.

"Okay honey, time for your nap (to a two-year old)."
"No."

James E. Billman

"Yes."

"No."

"Yes."

"No."

After so much of this, who is the child and who is the parent? Who is communicating in the above scenario? To borrow from the work of Eric Berne who was the creator of Transactional Analysis and the author of the best-selling book, *Games People Play*, there is a lot of role playing that takes place in communication. In the above dialog between a mother and her child, there's something askew when the mother assumes the role of a child rather than the role of a parent. To argue "yes" and "no" with a child puts the mother in the role of another child and subtly questions how one un-authoritative child can tell another child that it's time for a nap? However, when the mother assertively puts herself into the role of the parent, there is no argument; it is time for the child's nap. If Mother chooses to continue the dialogue and wants to talk some more to the child, she could follow with another imperative statement such as "It's two o'clock and you're tired," or she can put a carrot out there for the child—after the nap. As previously stated, we should not argue with a teenager or reason with a child, or is it the other way around? Either way, with young children the roles are clearly defined; the young, immature child is not capable of being anything but a child while the parent is the one with the option to choose his/her role.

In explaining Transactional Analysis, Berne included one more role, that of an adult. With three roles: child, parent and adult there would be nine possible ways for people to transact, and the transaction becomes communication when the two people interacting are fitted into the role that produces an optimal outcome.

Table 1: Communication Scenarios

Child to Child	Parent to Child	Adult to Child
Child to Parent	Parent to Parent	Adult to Parent
Child to Adult	Parent to Adult	Adult to Adult

For example, a mother effectively plays the role of an adult in talking to her twenty-year-old adult son, assuming he plays the role of an adult and not that of a child. Yes, he is her son, but no longer is he a child in chronological age or mentality; and yes, she is his parent but her son doesn't communicate very well upon hearing the parent because he has outgrown that type of communication. Good secondary teaching, in my estimation, would be the teacher in the role of the adult and the students also acting as adults; thereby removing the children from the classroom because they are a distraction and have no reason to be in a place of higher learning. Why is it so difficult for the gurus of education to understand this?

A student left the following note for me on the last day of my last term, and I quote: *"Dear Mr. Billman,*

I would like to thank you for being such a good teacher this semester. I have learned a lot from this class. I wish you would teach chemistry because I'm sure that class will be very difficult and if I knew you were going to be my teacher, I wouldn't have to worry about not learning. I really like how you treat us like adults (even though some don't act like it), and how you don't 'dumb things down' for us. Because of that, we know what to expect when we get older and into college. Thank you for everything, Mr. Billman."

My pride for this student knows no bounds.

In my obvious oversimplification of Eric Berne, it is important to transact in the proper role and to influence the other person to assume the same. In my example from above with the "mother as parent" and the self-proclaimed not sleepy "child as child," the relationship evolves over time. The next step in the relationship places "mother as parent" and "child as adult," and as her child matures it ultimately culminates in "mother as adult" and "child as adult." Sadly, as we grow older and less capable to manage affairs on our own, there are many instances in which another role change occurs as the once-child has to play the role of the parent to her once-mother who has become child-like.

Crosby, Stills, Nash and Young said it so appropriately in their lyrics to *Teach Your Children* ©

"You who are on the road must have a code you can live and so become yourself because the past is just a goodbye."

"Teach your children well, their father's hell did slowly go by, and feed them on your dreams, the one they picked, the one you'll know by."

"Don't you ever ask them why, if they told you, you would cry, so just look at them and sigh and know they love you."

"And you of tender years can't know the fears that your elders grew by, and so please help them *with your youth, they seek the truth before they can die."*

"Can you hear and do you care and can't you see we must be free to teach your children what you believe in. Make a world we can live in."

Teach your parents well, their children's hell will slowly go by, and feed them on your dreams, the ones they picked, the ones you'll know by."

"Don't you ever ask them why, if they told you, you would cry, so just look at them and sigh and know they love you."

-2-

Throughout this discourse I have made references to the parental influence that ranges from non-existent to unqualified to over-protective, and parent-teacher conferences are a prime example illustrating this range. Parents who show up for parent-teacher conferences are doing the right thing simply by attending the conference. They stand head and shoulders above those parents who opt out with the excuse that "Johnny's grades are good so there isn't any need for me to attend." Parents should understand that the conference is both communicative and collaborative just as much as teachers should understand that a conference is much more than a mindless grade review. Parents shouldn't bring their biases and prejudices, and teachers shouldn't assume the role of the parent. Conferences are adult to adult and Johnny, although we love him as a precious child, has to be somewhat objectively discussed in this instance

I personally didn't always approach conferences this

way, but did learn over the years to communicate in the two-way manner that I identify with teaching. In the years that I took part in these conferences, I had only one instance where a lady thought that it was my fault that her daughter was doing poorly; the reason for her daughter's poor performance was because I didn't like her. The accusation made me want to say something like, "Lady, I'm not here to make friends or sit in judgment of students. Although I may not approve of the way your daughter conducts herself and the choices she makes, I have no personality conflicts because we have no interaction at that level. I am a teacher (adult) and your daughter is a student who unfortunately is behaving like a child. When she leaves her assigned seat for no apparent reason other than to cause a distraction for the rest of the class, she has broken a rule and is reprimanded accordingly; when she fails to hand in her assigned work, she gets no credit; and when she sleeps in class, she suffers the consequences when tested over the material. I do, however, keep score so when her final grade reflects poor performance on her part, it is solely the result of your daughter's lack of effort in this class." But I didn't speak out because the mother stomped out of the room yelling about how she was going straight to the superintendent's office to make sure I would not be a teacher "tomorrow morning." This is a clear case in point where I wish the lady could have turned the tables and understood that she and her husband had always been and are now the primary teachers of her children, and her child came to class with an immaturity that portrayed both irresponsibility and unaccountability that should have been taught at home before her child was sent to school. Had the lady stayed and had I wanted to continue the pointless argument, I could have asked about her responsibility and accountability as well as about her personality conflict with *her* daughter.

No, I did not say these things or turn the situation around, but rather, sat there and let her vent. Had I acted out, I would have certainly been reprimanded; perhaps fired over being brutally and tactlessly truthful. This lady was the rare exception, and she had not come to the conference to find out why her daughter did poorly, but rather to put blame on someone else. I'm sure you can see the mother's influence on this child and why I profess the parent to be the primary teacher—the daughter was a carbon copy of her mother in the fact that their failures in school and in life are someone else's fault—another prime example of a parent exhibiting child to child behavior when her daughter needed something else.

Of course there were other incidents with parents away from parent-teacher conferences where my judgment was questioned, and rightfully so. In retrospective thinking, there are hundreds of cases that I didn't handle well, comments that were unnecessary and/or not very well thought out, and things that I did that I didn't go back and try to fix. There were equally as many incidences in being a parent, which is why I feel that parenting is a "here and now" thing and that it is ongoing requiring immediate remediation. Having survived as a teacher and a parent, the best advice I could offer would be to return to my earlier commentary on informal and formal learning. Build the informal relationship but don't forget to maintain it, remodel it and fix it before it gets worse, because if you don't it will only get worse. The formal learning will follow. Parenting is a form of echolocation; the way a bat or porpoise can find their way as they move about in dark or murky surroundings, it is two-way communication.

One more comment from my experience with the irate mother concerning her daughter: I did not informally reach the daughter and consequently failed to deliver to her the necessary two-way communication of formal teaching. I think that is why I sat silently as the mother vented on me—I *do* share my part in her failure and I *do* hold myself accountable and I *do* wish it would have played out differently because of the role I play as an adult teacher reaching out to students as adult learners. Perhaps, I had behaved too much like a parent in dealing with my student.

Just as I have searched for reasons concerning when and why so many students lose their interest in school, parents often do the same and wonder what took place to drive their child to no longer seek or react positively to their parental input. Peers, hormones, comparisons, angst, embarrassment, and other outside factors can compositely contribute to the rebelliousness and argumentative relationships seen between children and their parents. When and why such a fissure occurred probably isn't finitely measurable but would be more of a culmination of a series of events that did not play out quite satisfactorily for the child. It could have been the result of inconsistency, indecisiveness or a long list of other things—one or all of them. But one thing is certain: there was a time in every child's life that the parent or the parental figure was the most cherished, most knowledgeable and most important person in the world. The child is pliable and even though we may charge them with responsibility and accountability, we know that this is not always enough when

Reform School

they make choices for themselves. There are many answers because there are many situations that transcend time and space; each and every parent must actively seek the formula that shows prudence, conscientiousness, consistency and concern. Parenting is of the present, but because of our experiences as parents, we also have some foresight into the future. I wish I knew the answer beyond the fact that there are few simple answers to complex situations.

-3-

I once stood in an automotive parts section of a big box store and watched a man, actually an acquaintance, and his school-aged son. The man was a former student, and I knew that he was definitely a graduate of the proverbial School of Hard Knocks, thanks in part to a his family's background that prided themselves in having an independent lifestyle in what has become an interdependent world—a social condition prevalent throughout America primarily in depressed, rural settings. Otherwise, the man was no different than many of us in doing the best that he could with the choices life had provided. In this particular case, the man was looking at chain saws and the boy was raptly watching his father heft the saw and go through the motions to check its features, balance and visible durability. I could see the admiration in the boy's eyes for his father, his hero, as a line from Harry Chapin's "Cat in the Cradle"© came to mind, "*I'm gonna be like you, yeh, I know I'm gonna be like you.*"

Since I knew the father, I knew that as his son aged, he'd eventually be expected to use the chain saw to cut firewood that would heat their home. I also knew that school had been trying for the father and probably would be for the son for reasons not of ability but more because no one in the family had ever benefited from the opportunities education offered. In spite of their present father-son relationship, I wished that the boy wouldn't grow up to be like his father because today his father could eke out a living, albeit meager, and when the boy became a man he wouldn't find a similar niche 20 years hence.

    I taught from a chemistry book that warned its readers that they could expect to change jobs six times throughout their working careers; not change from one company to another company doing the same thing, but would change what they were doing to earn a living. And the kicker was that four of those predicted six jobs didn't even exist yet—they weren't even definable. Although extrapolated data, this was nevertheless thought-provoking.

    Here's the cold hard truth involving globalization: if someone can do your job and they are willing to do it for less money, they will. Weren't we warned 25 years ago with a similar caveat regarding robots: if a machine can do your job, it will? And it did. Parents need to understand this for the sake of their children and to emphasize the options made available by education. If I could say only one thing about the merits of education, it would be that it gives a person more choices in life. There is nothing that I know of that parents can give their children that will bring guaranteed happiness, financial success or health, but an ongoing emphasis on education does widen the options of choice for them. There are many people who, with little education, made the correct career choice for financial success; but there are exponentially a lot more folks who restricted their choices by not having enough education.

It was futile for me to argue with the students that were convinced of their future; who took a fatalistic attitude. "My Paw-paw (grandfather) was a coal miner, my Daddy is a coal miner and I'm going to be a coal miner so why do I have to know how many electrons there are in oxygen?"

First of all, the student's question was likely nothing more than a diversionary tactic to get me away from the lesson, and secondly, I couldn't give an answer that was satisfactory to the point that it would influence the student's thinking. There were occasions when I took the bait and answered these types of questions with the logic of offering choice to which the student would point out that he had made his choice—he was going to be a coal miner. What could I say other than, "Good for you, you're fortunate to know exactly what you want to do and I wish you well. I also hope a machine never takes your place." I could have pursued the issue and pointed out that coal mining isn't one of the most stable jobs and that mines close from time to time; I could have brought up the fact that mining doesn't provide the financial benefits for the good life; that the working conditions at best aren't good; and that mining is dangerous work. I could have rebutted him with hurtful comments too, but regardless of what I would have said; coal mining still looks pretty good to an invincible, energetic young man for a lot of reasons. His Paw-paw and his Daddy haven't provided the options of a wider choice for their children, even though both of them know fully the good and bad aspects of being a coal miner. I could only imagine a similar discussion in a classroom in an inner city, gang-ruled environment where the choices are even more limited. Yes, I could answer the question concerning the electron's importance in one's future endeavors, but not to the satisfaction of a student who had no concern and little knowledge of what is obvious in an ever-changing future. This is one more reason why parenting is a major responsibility and if that responsibility isn't present in the home life of the child, the school should not be held accountable. Yet in a bit of irony, these are the very parents who blame the schools. It is imperative to understand that parents are the primary teachers in their child's life, and there must be ongoing avenues of open communication.

I sometimes answered the question "why do we have to know this" another way, too. "There's the door, why don't you leave and go work in the coal mines. It's a free country. Get your parents to sign a release so you won't have to go to school anymore. Heck no, you don't have to know anything about electrons." I would smile when I said this, but it's obvious from what I have written that I was also serious.

If a student doesn't want to learn, he or she won't. Our schools are liberally populated with students that have no incentive.

With so many families strapped with the burden of simply providing room and board, it is tough for them to supply the nurturing aspect of parenthood necessary to raise children, particularly in spite of all the distractions of society. Many parents fail to understand that the responsibility rests squarely and totally on them. The shift in society has been so divisive to the nuclear family in so many instances that by the time their child graduates from high school, Mom and Dad don't live together in fully half the examples recounted. I learned to not assume the last name of the parent to be the same as the child, which isn't always detrimental, but nevertheless is food for comparison when examining the quality of school work between students coming from different familial upbringings.

Parental attitude toward education is important and the failure to make schools a big deal, a really big deal, doesn't bode well or mesh well for informal or formal learning. In my example, Dad should teach his boy how to cut wood and handle a chain saw, but he should also teach the necessity for achievement in school, partially due to the inconstancy of a dynamic society.

As in many cases, there are polar ends. My family was torn apart by the death of our mother when my brothers and I were quite young, but fortunately the importance of college was very high-priority stuff to my seventh-grade educated father. For all the turmoil that Mom's death brought, I shudder to think how much harder my life would have become if Dad had taken the laissez-faire attitude to his children's educational growth. As indicated, I fought it all the way, but when I walked across that stage with a baccalaureate degree on a winter night in Northern Iowa in 1966, it was my Dad and my step-mother that I was most proud of because it would have never happened without their badgering, prodding and constant reminding for me to keep trying and to hang in there. It was their accomplishment way more than mine.

But there's another item that parents need to act upon, and that is the need for an educational revolution to move the American public school curriculum toward a global focus for no other reason than to give their children a greater opportunity to meet the world head-on. It is also difficult to convince people, specifically parents, of this truth if they don't realize the effects that globalization has already had and will continue to have. The point has to be driven home more to parents than to children that if a job can be done more cheaply by someone else, by an animal, by a machine, by folks in another country or by a robot—it will be. Change is exponential and coupled with the Law of Entropy that governs what seems to be a fickle universe; what worked then might not be what works now, and what works now most likely won't work when (later).

Cutting edge education teaches with an international flair using the language of science and mathematics that provide us with the knowledge, among other things, of the eight electrons of oxygen. In each molecule's quest to fill its outer orbit, fires can burn, water can form, food can grow and life can exist.

-4-

I once took a class that focused on the gifted and talented learner in which the instructor mentioned on several occasions that "every child is a gift, but not all children are gifted." She repeated this phrase in order to make the emphasis that when dealing with a parent it is sometimes necessary to discuss why, even though their child is earning high marks on grade reports, he or she is not in the state-ordained classification that identifies gifted students. What parent wouldn't be proud to hear that his/her child is in this rather elite group for no other reason than for the distinction it brings, whether genetic or otherwise? In some cases it was distinctive enough for parents to openly reflect their own intellectual acuity, and rightfully so.

It's interesting to note that a gifted student in Iowa, for example, may not qualify to be in the corresponding program in another state or even in a different school in the same state as the criteria for inclusion are rather nebulous. In Iowa, the criteria were 1) to be in the upper 5% in standardized testing in any or all academic areas; 2) to be recommended by a teacher for extraordinary classroom achievement in the subject area, or 3) to be recognized as an outstanding musician, artist, athlete or leader. It wasn't just the eggheads and nerds in Iowa, but talent was recognized over a wide range and gave the program balance across the entire student body. It's also interesting to note in the discussion that many schools have seen the funds provided for the gifted student program diverted elsewhere and minimized the actual gifted program for reasons as goofy as not knowing how to implement it. This issue was often the discussion at Iowa's annual meetings for Gifted and Talented teachers and facilitators. On the other hand, the gifted program was totally different in Kentucky; to my knowledge, it was all but absent beyond giving teachers a confidential list that asked us to take this noted ability into consideration when assigning tasks such as homework, doing research, etc..

Later, as the instructor in the gifted and talented program when teaching in Iowa, the problem seemed to be that once identified, what does the school do to meet the needs of this group? It was like saying, here are the brightest (however not necessarily the most well-behaved or energetic) kids in school, so what are you going to do with them? The same question came from the parents of these students during conferences, "What can we do with Johnny or Shakena, they just don't have any interest in school, and I know they could get better grades?" It was a tough call, this "what to do" with them. Fortunately, my school gave the gifted program more than mere lip service and actually put these students in a class that met at least every other day, and the best part was that I was pretty much given a free reign in how to conduct the program and use the funds. Undoubtedly, I developed much of my present philosophy of education through my experiences with this group of students because they were the movers and shakers that the colleges were recruiting as well as the students who were going to find success in the higher reaches of academia. Nevertheless, it was quite a dichotomy of students that ranged from the high achievers to those who were "bored out" of anything that related to high school who assembled themselves in front of my desk for Talented and Gifted (TAG) class. I loved it!

The answer to making it a successful program came from mere involvement and through interaction in kind. Much to the displeasure of the proponents of "mainstreaming," for one period every other day we pulled these students away from other students and put them together, stirred the mix and evaluated what came out. I suppose that I could say the program was run under the "garbage can soup" theory with only one not-so-secret ingredient—involvement.

I mention the gifted program because in passing advice to parents from experiences that I've had as both an active and a passive observer of youth, it would be the need for ongoing involvement. It seems reasonable to say that involvement is the answer to the conundrum over when and why a child loses interest in school and/or when a child loses interest in heeding or even considering parental influence—that point in time when he or she feels no longer involved or becomes more connected to other endeavors. Call the something else peer pressure, call it an interest in something other than where the interest was yesterday, call it teenage angst, call it what you will, but I feel strongly that parents can affect their children's detachment from school and home life through ongoing involvement and that parents can also influence the direction they take. Nothing cryptic in that, is there?

Here's a list of suggestions about how one carries out that affectation in order to keep involvement in a child's life positive. Involvement includes: 1) direction more than management; 2) insertion more than meddling; and 3) participation more than presence. And as always, the medium is communication.

1) **Involvement is more direction than management.** Direction implies facilitation whereas management exerts control. For example, consider a major league baseball game where the pitcher is in a jam with runners on base, less than two outs and a formidable slugger coming to the plate. The first visit to the mound involves the pitching coach who comes out to talk with the pitcher in order to help settle him down as well as offer some sage advice. The pitching coach, the pitcher, the catcher and sometimes other infielders hold a forum of sorts—adult to adult communication. If the pitcher does not resolve the situation favorably, the next visit to the mound brings the manager, whose title fits him perfectly as he comes out only for the purpose of removing the pitcher and bringing in someone else to do the job. There's discussion, but the decision is foregone when the manager comes to the mound—neither the pitcher's feelings nor

his input are considered.

2) Involvement is more insertion than meddling. Salespeople are taught to get their clientele to say yes to a variety of seemingly trite questions before they ask the big question concerning the closing of the deal. As they make their presentation, the fact that there is communication is a sign that they are succeeding, and when the prospective customer is agreeing with the salesperson it is a sign that the negotiation is proceeding favorably. The salesperson in this case has inserted himself as a knowledgeable conveyer of information without relinquishing his position of influence. Conversely, if a car salesperson started a meeting with a prospective buyer by asking whether or not the customer thought he or she could really afford the five hundred dollar monthly payments that go with the car, the customer would find the question meddlesome and even rude. Like the trained salesperson, a parent must understand that if there hasn't been a foundation for communication built in the past, any attempt at insertion is going to go beyond meddling and actually become offensive. My best advice is for the parent to insert themselves in the manner that an adult would speak to another adult, and steer the interaction to remain in this mode.

3) Involvement is more participation than presence. There are parents today who boast that they have never missed an event in which their child has had a part, whether they were a tree in the first grade Christmas play or the twelfth girl on the junior varsity basketball team. That's an admirable example of being there in support of their child, but one of being present, and leads to the question of whether the same parents boast that they have never missed an opportunity to be involved in parent-teacher conferences? It is pretty difficult to actually participate in some extracurricular activities, but not so hard to participate in inter-curricular activities. By this, I mean the classes the child is involved with; things like science, math, history and English discussed, for example, around the dining room table. I've alluded to this previously, but there's no reason to not be involved in the classes one's child is involved with. So you can't do the math, have your child teach you, or having her refresh you on the subject might be a better way to put it. The old saw is true, if you want to really know something, teach it to someone else; plus if your child teaches you a lesson although you know it yourself, it indicates the child's mastery of the lesson. How would it hurt a parent to relearn the chemical symbols, to give up some television during homework time, to take a vacation with a historic theme? The opportunities are virtually unlimited. Don't merely send your son to a baseball clinic; in showing a mutual interest you're supporting the strong foundation and esprit you've built throughout his early years and now maintain through active involvement.

My message may seem as if I'm "preaching to the choir" by redundantly saying that parents are the primary teachers of their children, first and foremost. We all know that parenting involves responsibility and accountability and when parents interact with their children with the same message that they live by, there will be good results. Stay current with your child's changing interests, make learning at home interactive and never express a phobia unless you enlist your child's help to overcome it, and you'll feel better as well as having expanded your own knowledge. You're never too old to learn.

James E. Billman

    I recently wrote a course guide for the Continuing/Adult Education Department of our local community college and appropriately named it *A Refresher Course for Mathematics*. In describing the course in the school's flyer I mentioned that the course would focus on parents who would like to be able to help their children do math problems whether in elementary, junior or high school. I implied that it could be a drop-in and/or drop-out class depending on one's particular needs. For example, a parent of a sixth grader may not choose to come to the lessons covering trigonometry or Boolean algebra because it wouldn't apply. I announced that classes would be both theoretical and practical. Five hundred flyers describing this and all of the other courses that would be offered were distributed throughout the community. Obviously, some parents couldn't attend, some didn't need to be refreshed and many didn't look at the list, but the results were underwhelming when only two people signed up for the class, which consequently was dropped as a class offering. This spoke quite clearly to the lack of parental involvement that is so direly needed.

Reform School

Real Life Adventure #4

It was the palindrome year, 1991, and the site was an upper Midwest, large school setting. The educational gurus of the district had collectively put their heads together and decided that one of the goals of integration would best be served if students were given a choice concerning their school. Students could opt to attend other schools than the one closest to them and thus glean the special opportunities afforded by the school of choice—namely football and basketball, and vice versa for whatever it was worth. Just choose your school and hop on the bus.

The move didn't actually offer much in the way of opportunity, but to the contrary, contributed significantly to taking opportunity away—depending upon the context in which opportunity was viewed. There wasn't really a particular school in the district noted for its English Department, or Science Department or Equestrian Science Department for that matter. Nor was the accelerated school an option unless a student showed the precociousness necessary to be invited to attend. The significant achievement was probably best seen in the fact that the transportation department managed to get students delivered to where they intended to go on time. Also the move created more jobs for supervisors because the number of fights went up, there was more drug trafficking, and the main office was a revolving door of students coming and going all day long. And for reasons unbeknownst to analysis, there were more babies conceived by high school students than at any other time in the history of the district. Stress levels also rose as more teachers resigned than ever before at the end of the first term, no doubt because they were removed from their comfort zone brought about by the influx and outflow of a more divergent, definitely chaotic classroom population.

    The outlying suburbs and exurbs weren't affected by the city mandate because they were located beyond the city nestled in their own districts; and being smaller districts, they already had community heterogeneity. However, they did perk up their ears in monitoring the events of the open enrollment going on in the city when they heard of several blasts that resulted in some broken eardrums when cherry bombs were tossed in some waste cans. Actually, the shenanigans were concerted to take place at about the same time in two other schools as well, but in these cases a few cherry bombs were also thrown into toilets that resulted in some severely damaged commodes. The responsible students, fifteen of them, were very surprised to find that they had been fingered before the second bell of the day as astute administrators triangulated the guilty parties via their addresses—seems that they all lived pretty close to each other and ran together in a gang given a new name by the faculty, *the stupidos*.

    As the curtain rose for the school year 1991-92 at one

of the high schools in an outlying district within the city, all the proverbial "t's" were crossed and "i's" dotted. The schedule was set, the calendar finalized, teachers and students alike had their individual places to be for every minute of the day, the floors were polished and the rest- rooms spotless. They had contingencies and plans for all potential disasters: fires, earthquakes, tornados, epidemics, shootings, unauthorized entries into the buildings, electrical outages, chemical burns and even attacks by green aliens. The school was prepared for fights between boys, between girls, between ethnicities and between boys and girls. Everyone knew where to sit in assembly and when they would go to lunch. They had security cameras, security personnel and even formed a concerned citizens group with the freedom and the authority to help insure that everything went smoothly. They installed mirrors to see around corners, had plans to bring in drug-sniffing dogs, and put metal detectors at the entrances. They practiced bus evacuations, had fire drills, tornado drills, chemical spill drills and lock-down drills. However, on the very first day of the school year as the principal stood Napoleonic-ly in front of her office watching the 'droids file by, a phone call came from one of the assistant superintendents at the Central Office who asked about her plans for bomb threats. "Oh sh...," and the school year was off to another rousing, prescriptive, pin-the-tail-on-the-donkey start.

Now this particular high school principal was one who was pretty possessive of both her domain and reign when a well-meaning underling tried to infiltrate the inner reaches between her ears with a new idea or an improvised method. Uh-uh, no thanks. Woe unto the poor schmuck who might try to trick her

James E. Billman

into thinking that the new idea or improved method was her idea in the first place. Nope, she was way too savvy for that old ploy, too. It was her school, her way. However, if she had a few days to brood over a suggested new idea, sometimes—well, a little more than sometimes to hear certain teachers tell of her, she'd put her own spin on the notion and hatch it as her own. Certainly there are truly some principals who actually listen to their legions, who support them first last and always, and who share the meager wealth or accolade that might trickle down to them; it is just that this principal wasn't one of them. She was definitely the "sheriff in her town."

And now, when she finally thought she could relax a little bit and let the manifesto that she had created go to work, she needed a contingency for a bomb threat. Understand that this was in 1991 when the notion of blowing up schools was in its infancy, and most principals knew little of bombs and bomb squads.

She would develop a plan, and she'd do it right then.

1. *Evacuate the students using the same routes as a fire drill.*
2. *Assemble the students in the same designated areas as used for fire drills.*
3. *Teachers take attendance to make certain every student is accounted for.*
4. *Guidance counselors compile teachers' attendance reports.*
5. *Stand-by for the "all-clear" call or further instructions.*

She promptly sent the newly written plan to the assistant

superintendent at the Central Office with an addendum saying her school would comply by adding a bomb threat drill to the already bulky booklet of emergency contingencies. With the task finished, she thought that it hadn't taken that much time and was rather proud; the need was addressed, the issue was resolved and the problem was solved. She would inform the Department Heads to disseminate the information to their respective departments and speak to the teachers during the next faculty meeting.

Among teachers in any setting, there are certain percentages of those who will always comply with a smile, there are those skeptics who will always question with ne'er a smile, and there is the vast field of grazers in between. The percentages are fairly constant, but the number of teachers that fit into each group grows in proportion to the size of the school. Further, they were so easy to identify: the *"Compliers"* behaved like teacher's helpers as they would sit with their eyes up in rapt attention; with their two quart Big Slurpee containers, their spiral-bound notebooks entitled "faculty meetings" in front of them; and with their Bic pens poised and ready lest an item of information might escape them. At the other extreme were the *"Skeptics,"* the agnostics of academia with their eyes downcast in an overt gesture that they had no intention of participation. Some were grading papers, some were doodling, some were writing notes to each other and others checking out their counterparts of the opposite gender—all of them detached in one way or another. Over time, like hungry wolves, the two extremes melded together, found strength in numbers, and became a fact of school life. True in all schools, the principal had seen it all before. A person could scour the country and the findings would be consistent: the *Compliers* were generally females and the *Skeptics* generally males; the *Compliers* taught in the areas of the arts and languages and the *Skeptics* taught science, math and vocational education; not much else could be correlated other than the longer each group was together, the more polarized it became. There was an old saying that said, "If you want to teach to a tough crowd, try teaching teachers."

This principal was experienced and had climbed the ladder one rung at a time, but she was only in her third year at her present school so she found that she had inherited a rather formidable group of skeptics. One mildly effective method that she used to address the situation was to assign seats by departments whenever there was a general faculty meeting. However, no matter what she did there was a particularly obdurate biology teacher who for two years had been a kind of burr under her saddle. He had tenure and was further entrenched by being one of the local teacher's association building representatives in salary negotiations. He always seemed to point out what was wrong with administrative decisions but at least he did so in an intellectual, pragmatic, tactical manner that, to his credit, kept him above written reproach. He was what is known as a lateral leader among his peers and was not hesitant to come to her office concerning teacher issues. So in all fairness, she was beginning to appreciate the fact that he was thoughtful and professional in their relationship while, at the same time, often providing her with a little "heads-up" information. In graduate school, one of her professors had warned her about people like him, "Too smart to be a teacher, ha-ha."

Reform School

During their first year in the same school, he had irritated her to the point that she made him a "rover," which meant that he had no particular classroom that he could call his own but would have to travel from room to room pushing his books, records, lab materials and demonstrations on a cart. During the second year she assigned him to teach two remedial science courses comprised of students who had already taken the class and failed it. This arrangement persisted into her third year—the present.

The man really was what folks who understand teaching call a "gifted" teacher. Subject-driven, energetic, consistent, fair and challenging, he didn't molly-coddle his students or insult them. Students either laughed at his humor or didn't know that he had made a joke. He explained with metaphors and analogies using comparison and contrast, cause and effect and methodologies that sometimes found him standing on his desk and sometimes talking to his hand puppet, Luigi. And he had that air of cynicism about him to go along with just enough aloofness to make students see him as genuine. Good qualities perhaps, but none that made him a particularly popular teacher with the students. However, like most of his colleagues he was challenged by some students, endured by most and appealed to others.

At the ensuing faculty meeting, the principal gave each teacher the bomb threat steps and read the procedure to them as the *Compliers* followed along and the *Skeptics* wondered why she felt the need to read to them. Feeling the tension that went with every faculty meeting, the principal thought how educators appease themselves by reaping personal support from the positives and letting go of the negatives; she was, after all, a teacher's teacher in her role as principal.

"So we'll all mention the possibility of a bomb threat to our Homerooms and tell the students about the procedure for them to follow. Be sure to post this sheet with your set of Emergency Policies and put a copy in your substitute folder. Are there any questions?"

As she scanned the room, the biology teacher had his hand in the air. "Yes, Mr. Johnson." (Oh no, not him.)

"Ms. Smith, how will we know when the bomb threat is over?"

"By the directive. Number four says to stand by for the "all clear" call or further instructions. (Whew! That wasn't so bad.)

"Another question Mr. Johnson?" as his hand went up again.

"I don't think I made myself very clear. It will be easy if a bomb is found and removed safely; and if the bomb is real and detonates, we'll have further instructions; but what if no bomb is found or there might be more than one, how do we come to the conclusion that there are no bombs based only on the fact that we haven't found one, yet? I'm not so sure I'd want to tell my students to re-enter the building with insufficient evidence. It could take a long time to positively ascertain that there was no bomb in the school, and if the threat came in the middle of winter, it'd be pretty tough to keep everyone outside for very long."

From the same table, another teacher spoke up. "Wouldn't it be better to dismiss for the day? Tell everyone to get their coats and get out."

Reform School

The principal was visibly without a definitive answer, but held onto the "further instructions" clause in number four. "In some cases we can't cover all the possibilities and will just have to act accordingly. I hope the situation never occurs." (There, that should hold them.)

"Yes, Mr. Johnson." (Here we go again.)

"Would you send the kids back in for their coats if school were dismissed or send them home without their coats and homework? If it was a vibration-type bomb in a locker, simply opening a door could set it off."

The other teacher interrupted, "Seems to me that you'd call the police and get them here and make an "all call" dismissing school and never say anything about a bomb, at least until everyone was out of the school."

And now everyone started to talk at once as the teachers turned to each other and voiced their opinions. The principal had lost control, but had learned to let it go for a minute or two before trying to restore order. There were all sorts of statements she heard, ranging from how the students will cheer for a bomb to blow up the school to the pandemonium and panic that would surely break out. She heard one teacher wondering how she'd retrieve her car keys if she couldn't go back into the school.

"Okay, okay, let's bring this to a close. There's a lot of other work we need to do and many of you need all the time you can get. Quiet, please."

Order was gradually restored so the principal could speak. "We've had some good questions, and I will work on this and get back to you." (That's the way to go. That's what we're supposed to say when we don't know.)

James E. Billman

Mr. Johnson had his hand in the air. (Not again) "Yes, Mr. Johnson. One more question then."

"But how will we know if there's no bomb the next day if no one found one."

"I'll send you in and you can tell us one way or the other. Now let's get out of here."

Chapter 5: Others

-1-

Many of the laws of nature also carry over into the social sciences. For example, Newton's Third Law of Motion "for every action there's an equal an opposite reaction" can be loosely applied to the ongoing struggle in partisan politics. Ancient Chinese philosophy has persisted for centuries with its *yin yang* theory teaching that opposites are rooted much the way a wave passes energy in the form of peaks (crests) and valleys (troughs) through water. There are hundreds of examples that illustrate how balance is achieved through opposition. Physicists speak of matter and anti-matter and share their sense of humor in telling us that for every cat there's an anti-cat existing in another parallel dimension that lies beyond description and outside normal comprehension.

However binding natural laws might be when applied to natural phenomena, they often can be affected when applied to societal issues. Newton's Third leaves us wondering how we can move from place to place because every action in one direction would simultaneously evoke a reaction that would put us back where we had been. Thanks to something called friction, much of the reaction is changed into other forms of energy such as heat, sound, and light that allow for mobility. A wave consists of troughs and crests that, when added together, cancel each other, but when broken into separate components, they exert their influence in diametrically different directions. Yin and yang are not simultaneous, because it takes time for "what goes around to come around." Although we don't have to worry about being deluged with anti-cats or fear the sudden appearance of our evil twin from one of those other dimensions, there's pretty solid evidence that dimensions do go beyond human perception. But it's also a pretty safe bet that they won't enter knowingly into our lives in the near future.

It seems that as far as life goes, maybe we're not so special. DNA compositions are surprisingly similar between species, and the number of chromosomes characteristic to a species has very little to do with cognitive or prehensile abilities. As *Homo sapiens*, however, DNA coding is unique to each of us because of differentiation. In fact, we are so differentiated that we can't agree on the interpretation of laws, whether social, natural or divine. We even disagree to the point of fighting wars over them. Case in point is this: natural laws apply, they overlap, and they apply to society, but all natural laws applied to societal issues can be manipulated. Which brings me to the change needed in our schools; we've *yin-ned* long enough and now it's time to *yang*.

The study of opposites can be applied to schools, too. Antagonistic relationships are doubtlessly part of human nature and perpetuate the process when we put the factions within segregated circles. Administrators go here, legislators here, teachers here, support staff here, and students over here, but at the same time, "they" want "us" to think we are a team but have set us up as opposites.

I once interviewed for a specifically-identified job only to find out that the position really wasn't available, but there were other positions in the same field. The principal said, "What's the difference? It's still science."

Strike one.

During the course of the interview with the principal, he took a phone call, presumably from the superintendent, who must have asked him whether he was busy because I heard him say, "I always have time for you, I'm just interviewing a teacher."

Strike two.

I didn't let him get to strike three. While he was talking on the phone I mouthed out something that had restroom implications in it and left the building.

Institutions, organizations and namely schools everywhere understand the importance of working as a cohesive unit, but few of them practice it because they don't have a true understanding of organizational management. As a result, there are the previously-described factions; the *compliers*, the *skeptics* and the tight-mouthed non-committal *middles*, none of whom want to be identified as such, but have key-holed themselves because of the perceived treatment they receive. It is a tough issue to address, but schools can take a big step toward unity by considering the following suggestions: 1) removing barriers of caste, 2) distributing work loads fairly, 3) expecting attainable results, 4) rewarding achievement, 5) sharing decision-making, 6) creating a pleasant environment and 7) promoting intellectualism. Yes it is tough to address, but tougher yet if we do not implement new paradigms for dynamic accomplishment that will raise our schools to be among the best in the world.

1) Removing Barriers of Caste: Kindly excuse the cynicism, but the most important person in a school's system is not the superintendent, and the most important person in a school is not the principal. Could a school district function if the superintendent were a CPA, a lawyer or a politician? Could a single school function if the principal were a deputy sheriff, a drill sergeant or a minister? Could a school function if a teacher were replaced by an engineer, a writer, or a physician? Yes, yes and yes. Aren't we all teachers? I would find it very hard to recount how many times I've heard principals say that they were "too busy" to make scheduled classroom visitations because "something else came up." However, I've asked myself more often *why* they make classroom visitations in the first place. On the very rare occasions that a superintendent came to my classroom door, he never came in and sat down but stood outside motioning for me to leave class and speak with him. I agree that job descriptions and work expectations have to be definable, but I profess the need for collaboration and equanimity by making the job descriptions overlap. In doing this, I would suggest that *every administrator* in the district, from New York City to Weedtown, *teach at least one class every day.* I'd go even further and make that class the number one priority on the administrator's job description simply to allow these individuals to stay in touch with reality. They need to know because as it is, they don't. I also propose that *every teacher would spend one class period a day actively serving as another teacher's aide in a different* *subject area* other than their own in order for them to broaden their horizons concerning what goes on elsewhere. School board members, as hard as they are to find in many cases, should make a pledge to spend at least a half-day each week in the schools they govern in order to understand the trappings and operational mechanism of a school day. They should spend their time in classrooms, in lunchrooms and in the mix rather than walking the halls when they're empty or hanging out in an administrator's office. Parents should be made to feel welcome in the classroom at any time as long as they don't become a distraction; but rather, to be encouraged as active contributors offering their knowledge and experience whenever they can. We could inaugurate "a take your parent to school" day every nine weeks at a minimum. In short, open the schools to positive influences from the outside. Recalling the words of President Reagan directed to President Gorbachev in 1987 concerning the Berlin Wall, "Tear down this wall." We need to remove the barriers of office within schools and to bring communication within schools as well as between schools and their communities.

My earlier reference stating that a principal is often called a teacher's teacher is, in truth, hogwash. "Principal school" certainly devotes time to personnel evaluations, but most principals don't become principals because they were highly successful teachers. They become principals to get out of the classroom, to advance their status and/or idealisms, and/ or to qualify for the higher salaries in spite of the super-long hours that go with the territory. Rather than the now-existent principal visitation process of evaluation, why couldn't the members of each department evaluate each other under the leadership of the head of the department? This truly would be a productive example of teachers cooperatively teaching teachers concerning methodology and how to teach in their subject area. Further, this type of evaluation would provide opportunity for two-way communication, which would be far more valuable than an ex-football coach who has become a principal to come diddle-bopping into a classroom every 15 weeks or so, whether announced or unannounced. I once taught with a particularly candid teacher, also the head of the department, who commented that "anybody can put on a good dog and pony show for one period, and the worst teachers in the school are the best at doing it."

Is a superintendent then a principal's principal? Okay, I admit that there is a hierarchy that has to be in place, but results need to be the measuring stick of success and better results would come from more intertwined involvement by everyone in the school. Job descriptions should be defined with overlap.

2) Distributing work loads fairly: The most difficult thing for me to do in teaching was deterring myself from delivering what I believed to be a quality program in the classroom in order to do the "necessary" other things. I was there to serve the students and looked upon these distractions from teaching as serious occlusions that kept me from meeting my goals for my students. Teacher contracts include the nebulous "and other duties as assigned" clause that meant monitoring students before, after and in between class; going to meetings; covering classes for other teachers who were absent; administering standardized tests; sponsoring a class; managing a homeroom; meeting district writing standards; documenting teaching styles;

adhering to mandates for students with special needs; making reports and literally dozens of other things "as assigned." A typical day brought changes in schedules, conflicting events that took students out of class, shortened classes, questionnaires to be filled out and still more interruptions and detracting activities. Even to remove a distraction from class, I was utterly amazed by the paperwork and consequently the time it took; I could not simply tell the student to leave. Business and industry wouldn't put up with the counter-productivity that takes place regularly in the classroom. I admired the teachers that could roll with the changes displaying a *que sera sera* (whatever will be, will be) attitude, but I also wondered about the instructional value within.

Sometime, somewhere, more administrators will realize that not all teachers are equal in delivering their subject material to the students, whether in methodology, technology or in any of the other areas that make teachers different from one another. The classroom teachers who teach what are known as the "disciplined" subjects such as language arts, social studies, science and math usually have daily work to grade, labs to set up, and workbooks to oversee. Other teachers don't have these things—I don't see physical education teachers, music instructors, shop teachers or library science teachers taking work home at night or over the weekend. I'm treading on hallowed ground here, but there are also many classroom teachers who have plenty of time on their hands to play solitaire during their preparatory period. I just don't know how they do it; superior management skills, I suppose. Whatever the case, doing all the other things away from teaching drove me wild because I didn't have the time to get the "important" things done and still consider myself to be an effective teacher.

English teachers at one school where I taught shared my opinion so they petitioned the principal (a former English teacher) to get help. The help came from all the others of us finding ourselves having to give up our preparation period to read and assess English reports. One of the teachers in the skeptic group died from the daggers that flew out of the eyes of the principal when the "deceased" asked if the English teachers were going to help him grade math papers later in the week.

Yes, I saw a lot of solitaire being played on teacher's computers so maybe I'm just bitter because I didn't seem capable of having that kind of free time. To me, a typical school day was like jumping on a moving train going to an unknown destination starting the minute I walked through the front door. My best classes came from having time to think and to prepare thoroughly so I could engage students meaningfully. I was good at it too; I was lousy at all the "other duties as assigned."

3) Expecting attainable results: I stressed the importance of this in *Chapter 2: Schools*, but reiterate: Until the time when we get 1) a national curriculum, 2) a solid standardized method of measuring achievements and 3) the latitude to deliver it with a local flair expressed via a teacher's individual creativity, there will be disparity. Ultimately we need to aim high, but like they say in baseball, you score runs one at a time.

Goals are achieved slowly. Schools haven't deteriorated overnight, and they won't be on par with the world's leading schools just because we have a vision of change. It certainly hasn't worked that way in the past. Others will be forging ahead while we're catching up. Sequentially, we first we need a consensus, then a focus and then a plan before we can implement a new beginning for education that will bring us into the present. We certainly have that consensus because the majority of us know of education's woes. The focus, the agents that bring about the change, should be nationally representative of their locales and be teachers from the classrooms. The criteria for selection to the focus group would include such things as being 1) from the "skeptic group;" 2) driven with long-term achievement goals for his or her students; and 3) a teacher of passion that can bring hindsight as a vision of foresight. I say this because education used to be effective and these were the qualities of the teachers. The plan needs to be developed to a deadline within a short period of time, perhaps two weeks so that the implementation can be in place as soon as possible. Then, we need to make it work starting right away rather than somewhere out on the horizon of tomorrow. It should go without saying that we won't get it done by sitting on our thumbs or through citing widely digressive pockets of skewed success here and there. We can't afford to wait any longer!

How does this relate to the teacher and the personnel in support of education? The teacher is involved on one end or the other of the communication that comprises learning. It would seem that if given a curriculum guide for a subject that has been developed and amended nationally, a teacher could accept the fact that he or she will teach from it because this is what students are expected to learn. How to teach the material is entirely up to the individual, but all those folks who assess teachers must make it clear to those in their charge that there are expectations to meet.

James E. Billman

The number one complaint of administrators about teachers is that it is too difficult to get rid of the weak ones. While the teachers are setting standards of instruction, the administrators need to clean their house and revise their operation to include the "teachers assessing teachers" suggestion I made earlier.

Remember too, that once the schools have undergone reform, the students will have been winnowed by their performance (or their lack of performance) so that everyone is on task and in tune with the objectives set before them. If not, they have been placed in other programs designed for them to meet with success, or in extreme cases of non-compliance, they are gone. Every student will have the fact that "school is an earned privilege" planted indelibly in their heads just as every parent will know the expectations placed on their child.

The teacher is challenged to teach the objectives but is limited in teaching them only by his/her imagination. If the students fall short, they are likely to have to repeat the course or be dropped from the program, and that is for the most part, also the measuring stick for the teacher. If she doesn't measure up, she is replaced. Isn't that the way it's done in business and industry? How long can a worker sit by his work station and read a newspaper when he is expected to meet production? How many times could a postal delivery person dump the mail in an incinerator so he could go home and watch television? There's even a clause for overpaid professional athletes in their contracts saying that barring injury, they'd better be able to perform when the season begins.

These expectations for educators and for students are attainable and realistic.

I expressed puzzlement in the section above concerning how some teachers get it done amid bedlam and confusion and hinted that maybe they wouldn't get it done anyway, or even worse, had no intention of doing so. I've been rather critical of administrators and disdainful of students, but teachers must be held highly accountable to make the process operate effectively.

4) Rewarding achievement: I have never been a proponent of throwing more money at education as a cure for anything. It would merely be nice if teachers and support people were paid more. I feel that if those "extra duties" were taken out of a teacher's life, many of them would agree that the salaries they receive are within reason in view of being a public employee. Nevertheless, when the teaching profession is held accountable and standards are raised, so should the benefits due an educator.

My vision challenges students to achieve up to their level of competence and when they attain this level or show they cannot attain it, they go elsewhere as their aptitudes and abilities suggest. I've mentioned that if this changes, they should have the opportunity to re-enter another program, and on the far extreme if they can't conform to any program, they are out of options in terms of public education. These few are then society's problems and most likely that is what they will have become no matter what a school tries to do for them. We have harbored too many of society's problems under the auspices of calling them students for too long. They have knuckle-dragged down an entire nation's school system already.

Teachers in charge of a classroom of students who have

been trained in this manner are able to focus their attention on subject matter, and it becomes much easier to move the class from beginning to where they need to be when the class is over. Teachers need to be rewarded for this through salary, through cooperative efforts from administrations, by being given time to develop and consequently assess their lessons and by being appreciated. Many people also believe that by making it more difficult to become a teacher, teachers get better; I'm not sure of that.

In making suggestions concerning the accountability of teachers, it should be mentioned that many resources are readily available to help teachers, but they need to be trained to use the technology available to them both in college and on the job. It's hard to count the many in-services I sat through to show us how to use technology where the presenter got confused, where the technology didn't work satisfactorily, and where the meeting ended with something like, "We'll have this device ready for you by early next year so you can use it then."

As a teacher, if I had trouble teaching my students force vectors, with all the technology available I would certainly turn to the internet for help. Many places already have programs in place that can provide interactive lectures between stations that can alleviate specifically difficult aspects of certain courses. Iowa's fiber-optic network feeding every school in the state was a forerunner for interactive distance learning, but once in place, educators were slow to implement its merits. Why? It was one more thing added to their already too busy list of things that had to be done. Something new was added but nothing was subtracted, which has pretty much been our public school history

Reform School

since the days of the Ben Franklin Academies.

Technology can give students who find something very difficult a way to gain knowledge from a slightly different perspective. Schools can provide tutoring programs to their students via the internet for less cost than hiring a search team to fill a superintendent's vacancy, yet they hire search teams. Wireless technology is a goal for schools today but little is available to make its presence integral to the learning process.

Make teachers earn their keep, but reward them for having done so. There are plenty of people from the public sector who can watch the buses come and go, monitor the lunchrooms, hallways and restrooms and will do so for nominal wages. Instill a no-nonsense program of disciplinary expectations that brings removal and not attention to violators and my guess is that supervision could get less stringent. The number one complaint of students is that they are given no freedom, but are treated as if they were prisoners. If they were made to understand that they would have freedom when they quit acting like convicts, a giant step forward would have been taken. It comes through teaching accountability for self and responsibility for one's actions.

5) Sharing decision-making: There's an old saying that goes something like "you are only as good as the company you keep" that reaches into organizational management, particularly in those instances where the organizational chart is flat, where a lot of employees occupy the same tier. Schools fit that mold. The principal is placed at the top, and depending on size, the assistant principals are next; a few digressions to include counselors and the curriculum director follow; and then the teachers are placed on a line at the bottom. This gives the principal a lot of decision-making authority over a lot of teachers who are often seen as a single homogeneous group with similar needs. The teachers, however, teach a huge variety of subjects and really represent a huge diversity of needs from xylophones to welding rods suggesting that they don't fit so well on the typical management chart as seen below.

Chart 5.1

Principal

Assistant Principals

Curriculum Directors   Counselors

T   e   a   c   h   e   r   s

There are other concerns with these charts, too. Counselors often complain of their lack of authority to get things done, especially when a teacher brings a concern to them. I remember counselors often saying "I'll have to talk to the principal about that," which implies that the counselor is a go-between who enjoys no authority beyond being one tier closer to the boss. Many counselors feel like everybody craps on them, which suggests that maybe *they* need to see a counselor. In other words, if arrows are put on the above chart, they do not necessarily go from the counselor to the teachers, but they do go from the teachers to the counselor. Likewise, the arrows rightfully go from the principal to everyone else, but not from everyone else to the principal. The counselor might have, depending on the situation at a school, an inroad to the principal that's a little shorter than the teacher's. Because of this, a teacher uses the guidance counselor as a sounding board as much as anything.

My issue is with the placement of the curriculum director who indeed makes the above chart shift to the left and who certainly has an arrow directly to the teachers. But again, the arrow does not go from the teachers to the curriculum director and that skews the entire organizational chart. To further complicate the issue, the curriculum director seemingly has carte blanche access to the principal, probably as much as the assistant principal. This obviously elevates the curriculum director to a position of power he or she cannot wield with parity because there is not parity among teachers whose subject matter is so diverse.

A case in point that I frustratingly remember was the mandate to include all four learning styles (Mastery, Interpersonal, Self-Expressive, Understanding) in our lessons in order to reach all four types of learners and incorporate them into a *Great American Lecture*. (Another "new thing" picked up at some seminar that the curriculum director convinced the principal was really essential for the success of our students.) "Have your lesson plan for this on my desk Monday by 10:00 a.m." was the directive given to the teachers from the principal. Since this was an in-service day where school was dismissed an hour early so we could attend two hours of meetings and be given umpteen hours of work, the teachers went from the principal's meeting to our "Learning Clubs" to discuss our mandate in small group settings. My learning club consisted of a math teacher, a science teacher, a social studies teacher, a Spanish teacher and a music teacher. To keep the story short and to not denigrate the system too badly, the learning clubs were nothing more than "bitch sessions" that left the poor leader of the learning club at a loss when she in turn had to file a report to the principal about the sum and substance of the meeting. This comes back to my contention that teachers don't fit into organizational charts very well. The math teacher saw no way that she could make this work in the very objective world of mathematics; the music teacher had absolutely no clue how he could do things that hadn't ever been done in the history of the world; the science teacher (me) shared his insight by telling the others to go on line and Google it; and the Spanish teacher took the trophy for non-stop bitching throughout the meeting. This left our leader, a true inspiration and a master of double-speak to invent something plausible, which she must have done as she was still an employee at the end of the year. (Looking back, I suspect she was a double agent for the principal.)

    This is an isolated example of what happens when the curriculum director has too much access, and in this case, too much influence on the principal. In my estimation, the curriculum director's main function is to act as an insulator and cause the certified staff to which he or she is accountable to suffer the least amount of impact as possible. It is not their job to buy into every new program and force-feed it to teachers in a nebulous, confusing way with the perception that teachers are like birds on a telephone wire.

    In reality, the organizational chart of a school gets

misshapen beyond recognition and even suggests that it should be three dimensional or spherical if it is to be truly realistic. I believe the curriculum director needs to work with a consortium of teachers who democratically give him or her go-ahead support to enact anything new. And as before, when something new is adopted, something else should be abandoned. Perhaps the consortium should consist of the various department heads who generally are long-time teachers who recognize old methods with new names. I believe the position is also a two-way street and directives from last year that didn't visibly affect the performance of the student body can be rescinded. Share the decision-making so it becomes useful and consider the diversity from one department to another.

  The same can be said for the principals. It baffles me why one principal wants a certain report on his desk at 10:00 a.m. on Monday and another principal at a similar school in the same district doesn't impose expectations and put deadlines on her teachers. The first principal wants the report or you're on his list, whereas the second principal wants you to raise the standard in the classroom or you're on her list. We need to understand that the classroom is the main event of a school—first, last and always. Principals, if this will be their job after our schools are reformed, need to hold teachers objectively responsible for their classroom performance; however, not as teacher's teachers.

  Principals would do well to surround themselves with a cadre from the different academic disciplines and activities that comprise a school in making decisions. Yes, they are ultimately responsible for what does or does not go on in the school so it only makes sense to draw on the talents of others who are available before making a decision. This makes it truly a process of responsible, dynamic decision-making. After all, in a good and functional organization, the two-dimensional organizational chart is nothing but a piece of paper that hangs statically on the wall. If the chart doesn't work, it should be filed it in the round can.

6. Creating a pleasant environment: To a teacher, the sound of learning is the best of all sounds. Whether the sound is barely noticeable during an examination or a cacophony of on-task chatter during a laboratory session, a teacher knows that she has achieved her goal for the day. She has a difficult job, but she knows that she is equal to the task made possible by a combination of training, knowledge, experience and most importantly support. She is not afraid that her students will fail any more than a good builder is afraid that his roof will collapse when it snows.

A pleasant environment is the culmination of everything else being in place; the clutter is removed, the students are capable and the responsibility is shouldered. Given support from above, from below and from the side, schools can accomplish what they set out to do. All those little circles that define "who and what" necessarily disappear in view of a definitive, totally encompassing, perhaps amorphous group of dedicated professional educators.

Just as "business is business" a school needs to be run as a school, not as a parallel to something it isn't. It starts at the top with the top letting it be known that a teacher has only one expectation while everyone else in the building is there to support the expectation placed on the teacher. I know there are schools like this; and if I can believe what I've heard, there was one of these oases in the district where I last taught. Teachers who have this kind of support no longer need appease themselves or justify their efforts with the five per cent of students who care, the promise of Friday's last bell or remind each other to just "play the game" simply to survive.

7. Promoting intellectualism: Teachers choose their major in college mostly because of their interest in a particular subject. I have spoken about the influence that favorite teachers have on their students and feel that my choice of majors came as a result of both interest in the subject and my high school teacher. A few years later, my interest shifted because of a summer program that focused on physics, a subject that scared the bejabbers out of me in high school because the teacher scared the bejabbers out of me. Free of that negativism and dulled by the memory of poor performance in undergraduate physics, I found a fascination with the subject that took me beyond where I thought I could ever be. My undergraduate major in biology suffered, but my shift was to physics. (I really want to say that I "gravitated" to physics, but...)

There was a time long ago when teachers could join professional organizations and be supported by their school to attend events that promoted new findings in their subject area. At one of these I learned about the Star of Bethlehem and how its actual presence was supported by mathematics applied to astronomy. Over time, I have listened to lectures by physicists and cosmologists, and although I never became world renowned or even county or town renown, I learned more about my subject than I had learned in college, undergraduate or graduate. Once the seed is planted in fertile ground, the plant grows.

That period of time gradually faded into the mist as budgets got tighter and no doubt some teachers took advantage of an opportunity to get away from the rigors of school imposed on them by an unpleasant environment. Who knows? Maybe negotiating committees traded the right to seek enlightenment for a higher annual base salary, but whatever the case, subject-area professional development is gone; in fact it has never been known to today's younger teachers and remains only a memory to the old-timers. Intellectualism is not lost in schools today, but is something that a teacher has to take on alone through his/her own desire to grow professionally. "Yes, Mr. New Teacher, you can go to the National Science Teacher's Association annual meeting, but you'll have to pay your own way and you'll lose pay for any length of time beyond your contractual agreement of one professional day per school year. You say the meeting is in San Francisco? That's a long way from here, in Pensacola. Have fun."

Let this suggestion come as the last of the seven: How much more receptive would a teacher be to an in-service if the in-service spoke to their field of interest? Don't misconceive what I'm saying because these in-services really do exist from time to time. In Iowa, a specialist would sometimes come and all the math and natural science teachers would get together and talk shop. We sat around and solved math puzzles, discussed teaching conundrums and unprofessionally dissed students. A good time was had by all and we each took something away from the meeting that we could use to make us better teachers. In another state where I taught, we had the mandatory learning club mentioned previously that was arbitrarily chosen by someone somewhere who thought it better to cross disciplines. As stated, we were supposed to talk about learning styles and getting our students to write in non-technical, non-scientific language that a science student has no use for in writing reports and a science teacher has no tolerance for.

There's nothing wrong with knowing about four learning styles. There's nothing wrong with writing to different ends. There's nothing wrong with the Great American Lecture delivered unceremoniously to a bunch of droopy-eyed high school students at an hour of the day before the rooster has crowed. But here is what is missed: 1) Whatever you call it, good teaching is carried out unconscionably because it is what good, creative teachers are doing already, and 2) chances are that it has been done before under another name or acronym.

Teachers can also grow their intellectualism by advancing their global knowledge and applying it to their subject material, but again they must be given time to research and innovate imaginatively. And if they can't do this on their own, they need to be supported by their department via brainstorming and sharing information at meetings. In short, I'm suggesting that teachers be given time to advance in their discipline within the framework of their school day. Teachers call themselves professionals so they need time to practice their profession rather than only deliver it and consequently become stagnant. Those who make the decisions, from school board members and administrators to those great thinkers in the ivy-covered bastions of academe', need to re-focus so they become supportive of teachers in the classroom teaching traditional subjects in tune with today's society. So much of the line-item stuff of a school squelches intellectualism and forbids a time for allowing creative discussion and brain-storming when a teacher is lost in the tediousness of extra duties.

We talk of a level playing field; we need a level playing field to replace the uphill one that so many teachers now find themselves playing on. Once this is done, the bottom line falls on the teacher to meet the expectations given them, and if they can't do it, they can be replaced.

-2-

The vast majority of what I've said to this point has been based on my experiences and observations. Few of my ideas are new as much as they are common knowledge; we know that public schools are failing and the existing system is in shambles. We also know why: 1) the older an institution becomes the more top-heavy it gets; 2) the more we constrain someone, the less productive he becomes; and 3) although we know that giving a sense of ownership to employees is synergistic, we nevertheless refuse to do precisely that. We must candidly and thoroughly re-examine the structure as it presently exists in order to trim the waste from the statehouse to the lady who empties the wastebaskets and provide an educational package by true educators delivered to the people who truly want it.

So who's going to do it? I wouldn't suggest forming a committee of experts because the first thing that happens in these circumstances is for the higher-ups in education to turn to other higher-ups from other fields of endeavor who know less about schools than the people already in place. It is a vicious cycle;

a self-deprecating beast that eats itself. In view of the present situation, it would seem to be facetious to think that reform can come internally; that those in the higher echelons would openly admit to their own failures on a grand scale. Equally unlikely would be for them to relinquish their influence and to not only listen but to act on what they hear regarding reform from those in the classroom. The infantryman in the foxhole sees a much different war than the strategist at the Pentagon. However, until the higher-ups do listen and actively get involved in what happens in the classrooms, the educational slide downward will continue. As mentioned, Quality Management kind of fell on its face when the leaders sought input, got input and then "forgot" to process the input. In other cases, organizations prospered where they did listen and used the input advantageously.

Nevertheless, believing that mankind is intrinsically good, I am convinced that we can heal education from the inside - we can solve our own dilemma through reform and clear thinking by applying the old "physician, heal thyself" adage. The vast numbers of those in education believe in the system and are capable of admitting that the system is out of whack but haven't been able to mount a concerted effort for change. Comparisons to other nations, lower test scores on standardized exams, issues and incidents that typify education tell us that major adjustments need to be imminent. Just as Bill Buckner didn't purposely make an error that most likely cost the Boston Red Sox a World Series title in 1986, educators aren't bent on the collapse of schools. My experiences have led me to believe that the sense of stewardship is more powerful in most teachers than the sense of self-esteem, particularly in classrooms. Because of the difficulties in delivering quality programs throughout, good educators do not use their positions only as a lunch ticket, but as a way to make a better world.

-3-

Originally, school boards were established with good intention of having representatives from the district oversee school decisions with the best interests of the community in mind. By and large, citizens who serve on school boards are well-meaning, public-spirited individuals but there are examples where others have brought personal vendettas to the table. As times have changed through the oft-mentioned trend toward globalization, local school board members need to follow the directive to "think locally and act globally." In the last section, I suggested that many of these citizens don't really know what's going on in the schools, and they get their information from hanging around with the wrong crowd. The position has evolved into more than merely going to meetings, fielding a few phones calls from parents and listening to glossy C.Y.O.A. reports of success from administrators. Most members, if the school district is fortunate enough to have a contested election, run their candidacy on the promise to watch the finances. That's good, but it's not good enough.

Here's a case in point where good intentions went awry because there was a hasty decision that resulted from insufficient data. This scenario has taken place many times all across the United States as school board members were advised that scores in math and science were consistently regressing. In the ensuing discussions pointed toward the root cause in the declines, the members wanted to know what the minimum requirements were for students to graduate. Where I taught, and where I went to school, it was two years of math and two years of science.

"Well," a member said, "I move that we change that and require three years of math and three years of science."

"Is there a second?"

"Second."

"Any discussion?"

Silence.

"All those in favor of changing the requirements for graduation in both math and science say aye."

"Aye."

"All opposed, say nay."

Silence.

"Motion carries, 6 - 0."

Little discussion followed and what seemed to be a simple solution was resolved; give them more of what they need. The principal was instructed to make the necessary adjustments to implement the change. Next year's seniors were to be exempt, but everyone else fell under the new mandate—end of discussion, what's next on the agenda? However it wasn't the end to the problem but the perpetuation and magnification of it; because to everyone's dismay, the scores in math and science not only continued to go down, but now they fell at a faster rate. More wasn't better in this case but was actually worse because more students in the higher classes brought about a lowering of the standards that resulted in boredom for the capable students and more befuddlement for the already-confused students. Had a math or science teacher been asked beforehand, he or she would have easily seen that more requirements would not "fix" the decline because it was too late at the senior high level. Actually, the school boards should have seen that the solution would come with a more intensive math and science program at the lower grades. Make the teachers teach math and science to students who were being taught to be accountable rather than advancing products of incompetence, at any grade level.

Over time, the situation has become worse because that particular mandate has yet to be rescinded anywhere that I am aware, although scores continue to go down. Innovative efforts to meet the mandate have resulted in watered-down science and math classes bearing new names designed for students who were not held accountable and responsible heretofore because the graduation rate has been used as the measuring stick for a school's overall success. Today, students languish in third-year math and science classes having learned only how to "play the game" so they can meet a requirement that in actuality requires less of them rather than more.

I would dare say that had these school board members followed up on their mandate by visiting the affected math and science classes and seen that the teacher lowered the standard, corrective measures would have been taken. Again, science and math became too mundane for the better students who needed a challenge to succeed in a later course while beyond the students who had no clue. I would ask physics students whether the problems they were encountering in physics correlated with their work in math classes. More often than not, the answer was "no." I remember several instances where advanced math classes covered only one or two chapters in an entire quarter.

Reform School

Why, because of the faction of disinterested individuals who had no foundation to be in the class, did nothing but disrupt it. Simply put, school board members need to be actively involved in representing their electorate in two directions; to the public who supports the schools and to the students who occupy the schools. As it stands, the hapless, powerless teacher shoulders the blame for a bad decision made by a revolving door of elected officials. As often happens, more was not better.

-4-

Here's another situation that needs to be revisited, namely measuring success by graduation rates. To have graduated means that a former student is prepared to function at the next higher level or they can aptly apply their learned craft as a productive member of society. There should be no question about it, graduates must have met the performance criteria and exhibited the necessary skills to move on. For a senior class to graduate over 90% of the students who entered as freshmen four years ago is impossibly good in some places and not so good in others. But whatever the local demographics, to go beyond the expected numbers for one's area is to approach nirvana according to those who think this way. I don't.

Schools in educationally blighted areas that have been in decline for fifty years cry out to us for drastic measures of reform that we can no longer afford to ignore. Major cities having graduation rates around 50% make students victims of an apathetic population that has nothing to offer. This is huge, and closely linked with poverty; it's America's deepest, darkest problem yet educational leaders in these areas seem lost in a multitude of social and economic problems rather than including educational ones. Many places do little more than shake their heads when confronted with or about the need for educational reform as if they are resigned to its failure.

When a student drops out, there has to be a net for them to drop into—at least once. And there has to be a ladder extended for them to climb back up—at least once. When a student graduates, there has to be something for them to graduate into that makes it worth their while. Again, I propose that this can come about by insisting on students becoming responsible and accountable at an early age from parents of similar ilk.

In other places, thanks to some forward thinking and individual assistance from parents, advisors and guidance counselors, many students can now choose from various pathways to graduation, which has to be a step in the right direction particularly when the pathways allowing a cross-over are carefully monitored. If a student in a lower track has a real aptitude for poetry, then allow a cross-over, but don't allow it merely because her boyfriend is in the higher track and don't make the cross-over a total change. In short, design individual curricular programs based on individual student aptitudes and goals. Every student in public education needs to author his or her Individual Education Plan (IEP). This is all part of the ongoing need to change our schools into a place of serious business. With tracking, high graduation numbers can be achieved and students' needs will be met as they tackle life at the next level, and in doing this effectively and efficiently, a quantum leap will be achieved in serving the diversity seen in schools today. Guidance counselors will find their job a lot more challenging, but also more rewarding when they put a student into a program that both suits their aptitudes and points them toward a career based on individuality and competency rather than chronological age. Our schools will no longer be about getting students through a set of minimum standards and counting graduation numbers.

The entire process of graduation itself could also change. Some graduates would follow tradition as four-year products headed for four-year colleges while other graduates may have met the performance criteria for their course of study in two years and are now enrolling in a hands-on vocational program at a technical school. Existing factors today have precluded the possibility that all teens can jump through all the hoops of conformity. I heard that when I was in high school almost fifty years ago, but have seen little to change it for the better.

-5-

The case has been presented and the examples brought forth. We've waited too long for the reformation, and we've gone down several paths that have lead to dead ends. Because of this, we are running out of time and need to get it right. Thirty-five years ago science programs were identified by acronyms; there was IPS science, BCCS biology, CHEM chemistry that competed for a school district's favor against others such as ISCS, ISS, AAAS and PSSC to list a few more. For the most part, the movement was aimed toward a more inquisitive, hands-on approach to science.

I taught Introductory Physical Science (IPS) for over five years. Its basic premise was two-fold: how discovery and enlightenment were affected through experimentation. IPS is still around today, but not with the popularity it once had. It taught students to process data and to seek information through discussion and comparison by doing over eighty experiments throughout the course of the term using some rudimentary lab equipment sold along with a very concise text book. IPS was a good course if the student could keep up with the "Aha" discoveries and relate to the statistical processing. In talking to former students, they reported that they did like doing the experiments but most of them said they didn't know how the process correlated one thing to another. Non-mastery-type learners were unable to put it in perspective and slugged through it day-by-day when success called for an ongoing overview.

Most teachers today have not heard of the alphabet sciences or their counterparts in the other disciplines of education. Textbooks now are often over 1000 pages and packed with sidebar information, experiments and corollaries that can total over one million words. Many high school students have not read that many words in their entire lives and are offended that they have to carry the textbook around, let alone read it. Speaking of sidebar information, many adult empathizers worry about the damage done to children's backs in lugging heavy back packs on one hand and worry that our children are overweight and need more exercise on the other. Life is funny. One day an editorial cartoon in the newspaper sympathizes with all the homework kids have and the next day the same paper runs a cartoon that makes fun of kids that can't read. So it goes.

Education seems to be its own beast and not something that can be understood by linking it with other entities. It's not industry because the products are so different, and it's not business because it can't be measured in dollars and cents yet we continue trying to identify it in terms of industry and business. Here's another problem that lies in researching; laboratory mice or monkeys are not available on which to practice educationally based experiments. If IPS was a failure, it affected all those who took the course for as many years as it was in place. If the eight-pound text book of today is too imposing to be read, the student likewise winnows his or her chances to exhibit a competency in the subject. It is difficult to experiment with humans, and therein lays a major problem with education. Educational science has tried a lot of different things and new things keep coming, but they also keep going by the wayside only to be renamed at some later date and tried again adding one more frustrating failure on top of past failures.

As the pendulum swings back and forth, so goes education. Most people would be flabbergasted by the volume of information available that addresses education and its needs. Every student that seeks a career as a teacher has to write several papers that reference a positive educational end, particularly graduate students. They have to take statistics courses that allow them to analyze their classes' understandings, but will never apply because they won't have time when they are actually teaching. The research institutions themselves produce utter volumes of educational outcome-based blather that leads to programs like *No Child Left Behind* whose only good point was its national scope. Although *NCLB* confused virtually everybody it reached, it showed that everybody could be reached.

We need a reformation that will consistently reach everybody and will affect everybody individually according to their needs. In other words, the term "everybody" doesn't put them all in the same auditorium being subjected to the same lock-step delivery of a static curriculum, but it does offer an individual single program built for global outcomes. A phylogenetic tree comes to mind with all its diverse life forms as a tentative formula for success.

In recapitulation, we know that the woes of education today are the woes of society tomorrow. It is not enough to send kids to school in the morning and expect them to come home enlightened at night.

- Education has neither changed with the needs of those being educated nor has it provided enough opportunity for diversification.
- Just as educators are not a viable group to fix the ills of business and industry, leaders of business and industry are not viable groups to fix the ills of education.
- Educational reform must come with educators looking outward from the classrooms as much as from the outside looking in.
- Teachers must teach and be held strictly accountable for teaching performance standards; they should not be enslaved to ancillary duties.
- Educational reform should result in a standardized approach to a global education delivered with a local flair.

Reform School

Real Life Adventure #5

<u>Remember This</u>

Written by: Stevie George, Age 16

It's been three years since we last talked, eagle.
There were times that I felt weak and feeble.
Yes sir I understand, I've been there too;
5 years have passed and yet I still feel blue.

Some people still don't believe it's real,
the day hatred brought down concrete and steel.
One day you think you can make it through
then you see something that brings it all back to you.

But I see we are here for the same reason soldier,
to pay respect for those that couldn't get older.
The day that pride reached far into the sky,
the day HERO was spelled F-D-N-Y.

I bow my head for each that died.
They all had fear, yet into death they stride.
These men were like no other, had no doubt
to run into hell, while everyone else ran out.

James E. Billman

Each of these men wanted nothing more
than to get every single person out of the door.
They gave their lives to let a stranger keep theirs.
The elevators were out, they climbed the stairs.

They checked every floor for signs of life
while thinking about family...their kids...their wife.
Some knew they would not make it out,
but they fought, and moved on, finding a route.

Then came the sound of it all crashing down.
It was real now, and in the dust they were drowned.
But they moved on, looking for a hole,
some clenching tools, some...their soul.

America had rarely seen such bravery.
Why eagle only a few flags do I see?
The minute we lose hope, and lose respect,
the terrorists have won, and we can't get that back.

America really needs to start showing its pride
like it was on 9/11...it should have never died.
It seems a lot has been taken for granted.
Many people's views have become quite slanted.

If we lose touch with what bravery made,
The souls of these firemen will slowly fade.
If we let them fade, then we start to forget.
When we start to forget, it becomes a threat.

The soldier with his hand still on the wall
got down on his knees and started to crawl.
He closed his eyes and ran his fingers
along each and every name...the pain still lingers.

Reform School

"My brother was one of these, eagle...you know my plight?"
"Yes" said the eagle, "they are all your brothers tonight."
You stand here before me in your uniform
military, police, fire department...you are all one".

The soldier then got back to his feet,
squared himself and brushed the dust from his knees.
He smiled at the eagle and said to him "Sir,
you are a great friend, I hope we talk more.

The soldier put his hand back on the wall one last time
as the bell at St. Patrick's started to chime.
He did an about face amid a thunderous crack
the FDNY memorial now at his back.

As he and the eagle started to move away,
something happened I can't explain.
Time seemed to stop in suspended motion.
People stopped mid step, apparently frozen.

And as this story was related to me
the soldier and eagle continued to see
the scene lost its color, just black and white.
Yet coming from behind them was a light.

They both had a tremble as they turned to meet
over 100 firemen standing in the street.
They were in good company, no reason to fear
as soldier and eagle shed a single tear.

The soldier and the eagle both raised a salute.
It was silent now, the world on mute.
Just then the soldier's brother stepped out.
"Thank you brother, it's what we're about.

James E. Billman

We gave our lives, so thousands could live.
All you have to do is never forget".
The two brothers then hugged, an eternity it seemed
and the others bowed their heads in reverent esteem.

Then they all saluted back, until the two dropped theirs
but none could stop or hold back the tears.
"I love you brother, thank you for this,
There isn't a day that you I don't miss."

Then all the heroes began to slowly fade
smiling as they disappeared in the shade.
The soldier or the eagle said nary a word,
still in shock of what they saw and heard.

As they walked quietly into the sunset,
the soldier and the eagle we can't forget.
The soldier watched the eagle take wing,
soaring overhead. Let Freedom Ring.

Stephanie's mom was a self-described flower child of the 1970's and her altruism from then is still evident today despite plenty of contrary experiences. She had Stephanie at the age of forty-one and knew from the start that she could do the job better alone than with Stephanie's father staying around. So it was, mother and daughter sharing their lives and forming a relationship held together by the bonds created by love, trust and communication. They laid it all out there for the other one to see; nothing would tear it asunder. They had their good times and not-so-good times like everyone, but endured and remained in a solid relationship throughout.

Stephanie was home-schooled until she was ten years old

when she, by mutual agreement, enrolled in the public school as she started the fifth grade. Very few of her classmates knew her so she found it difficult to reach out to others in order to make friends. At first Stephanie was somewhat wary of the others and when the opportunity arose for her to mingle; she did not feel that she had much to offer. As the cliques from past years quickly re-formed, she was very uncomfortable inviting herself into any of the small groups of girls. Stephanie, uninvited and developing a defensive attitude, became a loner. And without allies, it wasn't long until she became a target. Whether a young school-aged person says it or not, school is made much tougher without the security of friends to buffer a person from the other unseemly factions and influences. Caste systems are built and perpetuated for many invalidated, unmerited reasons ranging from the ever-present bullying groups to the brand of clothes a person wears. She wanted to quit school but her mother wouldn't allow it saying that public school was what they had agreed, and she would have to do her best to make it work.

There were other instances that set her apart, too. Stephanie had never so much as seen her father until the day he showed up at school and demanded to take Stephanie with him, to virtually kidnap her. Unfortunately the incident took place in view of all the other students in her class and served to demean her even more. A man showed up at the classroom door unannounced and asked the teacher if a Stephanie Fox was in the room. He said that he was her dad and wanted Stephanie to come with him. As all eyes immediately turned toward her, Stephanie sat both mortified and frozen in her seat. She had no look of acknowledgement on her face and obviously appeared reticent to leave her seat. The teacher was equally dumb-struck to the point of not knowing what to do other than to resolve the incident as quickly as possible and consequently told Stephanie to leave the room and go with her father. The teacher thought that surely the man had cleared himself by reporting to the school's office before coming to the classroom. Although in retrospect, she could not recall having seen a visitor's badge around his neck and admitted her error.

Still, Stephanie sat transfixed at her desk. It was only after a boy behind her gave her a shove and in a loud whisper said, "Well get up, stupid."

So she found herself walking down the hallway with a man she had never seen, a man who had informed her only a minute ago that he was her father and was now taking her to a place unknown. Fortunately for Stephanie, this man had done the same thing in some of the other classrooms; he had knocked on the door and asked for Stephanie Fox. This aroused a degree of suspicion in one veteran teacher who contacted the office causing Stephanie and her so-called father to be intercepted by the principal as they came down the hallway to leave the building. The principal had also been in the profession for a long time and held no reservation in taking the offensive wanting to know "Just what is going on here? Stephanie, you know that your guests need to come to the office when they come into the building and that you're supposed to come to the office to sign out if you're going to leave the building."

The principal asked Stephanie's father his name. His only answer was the answer he had already given, "I'm Stephanie's father, and I come to take her with me."

Reform School

During the exchange, an administrative staff person walked up and told the principal that according to Stephanie's personal data sheet the only person authorized to come for Stephanie was her mother.

"Sir, you're not on our list. If you take this girl out of this school, I will immediately notify the Sheriff's Department and you will be arrested. If you would like to wait, I will call Stephanie's mother. When she comes to the school to personally say this is okay, then Stephanie can go with you."

The man decided not to wait but to "come back later" as he beat a fast retreat. To this day, there is only the assumption that this man was truly her father. Stephanie was sent back to class and had to endure the mean boys' taunts at lunch. "You don't even know your own Daddy. You're so ugly you scared your Daddy away."

But, there were a few good things that came from these times. The singular most significant event of her first four years in public school came as a result of a literature class in eighth grade when her teacher recognized a raw, but repressed talent in Stephanie. He saw that she had the ability to compassionately convey the human condition and could do it in verse. Stephanie was a poet. He praised her efforts and as a result, he kindled the inner flame that had lain dormant for all this time. Befuddling in a person so young, Stephanie showed a deep understanding of events far removed and could capture the intricate emotional feelings that went with the events. Asked how she knew so much, she merely responded with, "I listen to people."

Otherwise, as time passed, Stephanie pretty much stayed to herself befriending two other girls who were mostly like her in the respect that they were also loners. When junior high graduation rolled around, Stephanie had distinguished herself to neither teachers nor peers. With her mother's counsel, she decided that she would look forward to a new start in high school and welcome the opportunity to be among new faces that the much larger high school would bring.

    Not being athletically inclined, she was attracted to the Junior Reserve Officer's Training Corps (JROTC) that was active in the high school. Based on military codes of honor, the program offered discipline, accorded mutual support among fellow participants and promoted a respect for country; all of which strongly appealed to her. She thrived both in the formal and informal aspects of the program and particularly liked Drill and Ceremony. Contrary to what the mean boys from fifth grade may have said, Stephanie was far from ugly and possessed the natural good looks that needed no enhancements; plus she was in the process of adding to her attractiveness through the self-confidence resulting from the JROTC program. She tried out and was accepted to be a member of the school's prestigious and highly visible Honor Guard that represented the Colors in both competition and at many of the school events. Stunning in her ROTC uniform and with a now-present smile that would melt snow, she no longer attracted the remarks of the mean boys but found favorable acceptance from other boys.

    Still retaining the scars from grade school, Stephanie was not outgoing but did enjoy the recognition she was receiving. Remembering the bad times from the past, she picked her friends carefully. In class, she suffered the difficulties from not having previously mastered the subject material that had been taught.

She did not excel in ninth grade English Composition where the subject materials were picked for the class and her self-expressive skills were held in check. Her grades were average at best. To her discredit, she retained an acerbic attitude developed by previously being shunned and seemed to be bent on "showing all of them that she didn't need them," which brought out a reaction in some of the teachers and students she encountered.

For no apparent reason, one teacher who reacted negatively to Stephanie was the enlisted member of the JROTC program in charge of the Color Guard. No doubt constructive at the onset, he became relentless in his criticism of Stephanie and the other three members of the Color Guard. Even though they performed well in competition and often placed first, it was never good enough for him. The shine of every competition, of every presentation was quickly dulled by his overly critical remarks. As a result of the acquired nature of Stephanie's rebelliousness, she announced that she was through with the Color Guard and not willing to consider that perhaps the criticism came because she was "worth it" in his eyes.

During the year, Stephanie and one of the boys from the JROTC program were mutually attracted to each other, and they started to spend some time together in school. He was older, had his Driver's License and started showing up at Stephanie's house as a frequent visitor which seemed okay—for a while. After a period of time, the relationship stagnated. She wasn't ready for the entanglements of a physical relationship thanks to some long conversations with her mother, and furthermore, Stephanie and her boyfriend had nothing in common beyond JROTC which made it hard for them to converse. He was all about his truck, his hunting and fishing exploits and his friends while she was more of a platonic nature. Stephanie told him that she did not want to have a boyfriend-girlfriend arrangement any longer and that maybe they could just be friends—an abomination to a teenaged boy worse than death.

    The rest of the school year quickly went south as the ex-boyfriend turned his friends against Stephanie, told lurid stories about her sexual behavior and spread all sorts of untruths about her that even brought her mother into the picture. Stephanie was jostled in the hallways, physically slammed against lockers, and was once pushed down a staircase so violently that she fell. She had her books knocked out of her arms on several occasions and was once again taunted, but this time more viciously than ever—all of it over her proclamation of not wanting a premature relationship with this boy. When her mother saw dark bruise marks in the shape of fingers on Stephanie's upper arm, she felt no recourse except to intercede. Stephanie knew that her mother would make it worse and implored her mom not to say anything to the police or the school, but finally agreed that if her mom spoke to someone at school it might help alleviate the situation. What it helped was to make it worse because as Stephanie had predicted, the school counselor mindlessly talked to the ex-boyfriend and a few of his cronies who only turned the table around and made Stephanie appear to be the perpetrator of the falsehoods. Had the counselors looked into the matter more deeply, they would have seen that Stephanie really didn't have much of an audience beyond a few close friends to which she could turn.

    While all this was going on, two of her friends announced that they were in a gay relationship that became further fuel for the fire among the ex-boyfriend's group. Mercifully, the school year came to a close with the only bright spots coming early in the year when along with being named to the Color Guard, she had written a poem in honor of Vietnam war heroes that was published in the local newspaper along with a picture of her presenting a beautifully decorated cake that she had baked to the commanding officer of the local National Guard Company. A teacher nominated her for the "Student of the Week" honor.

The next August, with new resolve, Stephanie re-enrolled in JROTC and was once again named to the Color Guard. She hoped the non-commissioned officer in charge (NCOIC) would be less critical and more constructive in view of the fact that a new officer had taken charge of the JROTC program. After taking first place in their division at the first competition of the year, performing much better than any other school, the NCOIC got them together and told them how poorly they had performed and spoke of the embarrassment he felt after working so hard. He closed with the admonishment for them to sit down and watch the next group, from a different division of the competition, "and see what a real Color Guard looks like."

Stephanie had also enrolled in a Creative Writing class and was looking forward to it with the hope that, for once, things would go better for her with the onset of a new school year. Perhaps the ex-boyfriend, now a senior, would have cooled down and everyone could get on with their lives. Two visits later to the school convinced her mother that nothing had changed. Stephanie had had her fingers smashed in a locker door, been detained from getting to class on time and been "felt up" as she had been pushed around in the middle of a group of boys.

When her mother made Stephanie show the physical marks and bruises to school authorities; they claimed that there were strict regulations against bullying. "Surely your daughter would have received her injuries at some other place than at our school."

At first, the Creative Writing class consisted of extraneous reading and discussions with actual writing assignments to follow. Stephanie wrote a poem and was pleased when she was asked by the teacher to read it in front of the rest of the class. Fully satisfied that she had read well and that the poem was one of her best, she sat down only to hear her work being torn apart by the teacher for having no substance, for lack of understanding, and for absence of poetic value. This was the proverbial last straw. The next day Stephanie and her mother came into the office, and she quit school. No school official asked her why; it was just "sign here."

This was just one more of a myriad of cases where a student finds no opportunity at school; where the detractors perpetuate their influence through sheer numbers and actually make it through a system without accomplishment. This story, like all of them in this book ends well, however. Stephanie had learned that there is no requirement for enrollment in a community college that calls for a high school diploma if the student is qualified to handle the classes she will encounter. Stephanie jumped through the hoops, got a General Education Diploma (GED) and enrolled in the college.

Chapter 6: The Fix

-1-

I began this book by mentioning that our individual knowledge of education limits us to our first-hand in-school experiences and to the information we have gathered through other sources. Having neither attended inner city schools nor taught at any of them, I have to rely on the information that comes from other sources and sort it for myself. Whether subconsciously or not, sorting the information makes it biased. Like most people, however, I have concluded the situation to be bad enough that the few reports of positive exceptions making the evening news serve more to substantiate my conviction than to reverse it. More often, we hear of threats for whole schools to be closed if they aren't meeting expectations, particularly the expectations of *NCLB*. This makes me wonder where the students from the closed schools will re-enroll; supposedly they will go to any other public school. After all, the latest mantra of edu-speak phraseology seems to include the catchy "Every child, every day."

Recently, a battle regarding teacher tenure raged in our nation's capitol between the teacher union and the District of Columbia's Superintendent of Schools. Essentially, the superintendent proposed a virtual doubled salary for the teachers if they would forego tenure. Many of us in the mostly untenured working world would jump at that opportunity, but in this case, there was a devil in the details. In giving away the job security of their tenure, teachers would open themselves up to being terminated based on their performance evaluation.

The media spin put on the proposal made it sound as if the teachers were quite complacent and satisfied with both their position and their notoriety in being a part of one of the very worst school districts in public education. It seems that in other states, where it is legal to strike, public school teachers go on strike for wages and improved conditions, and some of these struggles between the school boards and the salary negotiators epically portray the teachers as callous and selfish. To the general public this smacks of being unprofessional if one is unwilling to be held to a standard of performance that is designed to improve the educational opportunities for students. It sounded as if the unionized Washington educators weren't interested in educating at all. My goodness, a doubled salary for these teachers would take most of them into a six-figure income range. Are they so fixed that money can't buy change? Are they afraid of the challenge of proving themselves?

For the teachers to trade tenure for money is not as scary to them as the trepidation that comes simply from not knowing what "a new and revised" performance evaluation might include or how it might be handled. Further, the teachers couldn't help but notice that they were being given total blame for the failure of the District's system and would be offered as sacrificial lambs to the disgruntled public. We all recognize that, regardless of the profession, if an evaluator wants to fail someone, it's pretty easy to do. Once these teachers relinquish tenure and agree to base their livelihood on the evaluation of a slash-and-burn principal who has a full time job without doing evaluations, let alone the subject expertise to evaluate, they perceived troubled waters—and rightly so. What's the wisdom in getting paid twice as much if you get terminated at the end of the first term? How do you all at once bring the performance standards up to *NCLB* standards if the school has never been close in prior years?

I'm no fan of the unions in today's market unless they become global in order to level the playing field. This, of course, will never happen without a legal enactment and humanitarian embracing of the Golden Rule into an international law. Unions had their time and their purpose when they represented their members against exploitation, but today some of them have become the exploiters. I do not care for tenure either, but in this case the union's rejection is a good decision on the part of its member teachers. However, I would hope the union's representatives in this case express enough interest in the offer to at least bring it to the table for both clarification and further negotiation. We may never know the outcome without an in-depth search because this issue is only a small pocket in a big nation where each state has its own definitions of education. The issue was news-worthy; the outcome is "who cares."

However, we definitely do know that we cannot condone the present conditions of the schools, and we also know that we can't go after the teachers with an axe as if they are the sole reason for the failure of the schools. Once again, it is a case of a team of horses with each horse going in a different direction that consequently makes the buggy late for school—or never get there.

In whatever denouncement of the existing system this text has presented, there are long-standing examples that reach to the other end of the bell chart, too. I have a dear friend who spent much of his teaching career in an upwardly-mobile, quite affluent school district that prided itself on the accomplishments of its students. Not that this system was a teacher's utopia; my friend related that some of the student's allowances exceeded the teacher's earnings, and the teachers were sometimes considered "just" teachers as if they were no more than a tread on the stairway to success. Nevertheless, the emphasis was placed on providing opportunities for achievement reaching beyond general education. The parents expected such things of their school because they expected their children to do well academically and qualify for entrance into prestigious universities. In other words, there was a big spread between this district and one where many of the graduates went to community colleges as first-generation students.

My friend, I'll call him "Joe" because that is his name, enlightened me about a program in which he was involved called the *International Baccalaureate Programme*. (I have made allusion to it previously.) Although not well known to the masses in public education, the program has been around a while being offered in three different languages and boasts of world-wide participation involving over 600,000 students focusing exclusively on classes of higher learning. In a nutshell, the *International Baccalaureate Programme* might be called a global Advanced Placement (AP) course with social and personal implications encompassing virtually every educational mission statement imaginable. *IB*, as it is known, advocates learners to be high achievers by extolling them to be: Inquirers, Knowledgeable, Thinkers, Communicators, Principled, Open-minded, Caring, Risk-takers, Balanced and Reflective. To paraphrase it slightly, their mission is to produce internationally minded people made possible through a worldwide learning community.

Included in the *IB* umbrella are the following discipline groupings: Language, Second language, Individuals and Societies, Experimental Sciences, Mathematics, Arts and Electives all of which are topped off with a 4000+ word extended writing essay. Not every student involved takes the program *in toto* but may opt for a class's availability and preference which is what the students in Joe's class did as he taught both AP and IB English.

So why not institute a similar national program, but in terms of being a bit more oriented toward a general education curriculum? Once we get off the track of K-12 and its few auxiliary lines to alternate diplomas by focusing more on school-to-work programs, our educational system would flourish with the creation of more direct pathways to success.

I might add at this point that I am continually haunted throughout this entire treatise by how it might strike readers that I have too lofty an expectation, and I cater to an audience beyond the capabilities of average students. Again, it is my feeling that once we get our schools focused toward challenge and once we re-invent and subsequently enforce a disciplinary code of minimum tolerance, we will be amazed at what our "average" school-aged children are capable of. My proposal is not a program designed

James E. Billman

for the privileged elite but one of choice pointed to all. I also feel we can do this abruptly, without much more than a summer of accommodation. Maybe not as simple as saying "Here it is, kids," but we don't need it to be a lot more difficult than getting the word out and then following through in its implementation.

-2-

In preparing this book, I often browsed school districts on the internet and read their mission statements. I would guess there to be over 20,000 of them; here are three, one each from Colorado, Indiana and Kentucky:

- *--- promotes student success by engaging all members of our diverse community in an atmosphere of higher learning, building upon achievements and replacing inequities with opportunities. The --- student will connect, contribute and compete in today's global society.*
- *All students graduating from --- will be prepared both academically and socially to become positive and productive citizens. The focus of --- will be to engage students and involve parents to create a community of learning and achievement.*
- *To reach every student, every day. We respect all, encourage others, act responsibly, commit to success and we honor honesty.*

Care to guess which one came from where? I can see a little urbanization in the first one (Indiana) to go with the alliteration, and I particularly like the global reference. The second one (Colorado) also comes from a large population center; in this case, I would guess that English as a Second Language (ESL) would be a course taken by a majority of the students. I'm taken with the school's recognition of the importance for parental involvement. The third mission statement (Kentucky) is very rurally located and quite honestly admits to having issues with student behavior. In simplicity lies its beauty, although I would proofread it a little more closely before having it represent my district.

They're all good. They are, no doubt, the result of a concerted effort on the part of each school wanting to develop autonomy in their separate districts as well as to address commitment and achievement. If I could propose a national mission statement for all schools it would go like, *"To develop people with functional ideas of self, society and the world."* as the principal objective of every school—nothing more. If students leave school with new or renewed ideas, they are capable of having met all those other lofty goals of the mission statements.

Throughout my career in the classroom I have somehow been fortunate to have attracted the so-called "weirdoes" as a sounding board for their innovative ideas. I've seen plans and listened to descriptions for levitation, for manure-burning cars, for vehicles whose motion creates power to sustain that motion (perpetual motion), and for thermocouples to power city and highway lights just to name a few. I heard students talking about biomass energy before biomass was a word. I've had conveyer belt highways described to me as well as uses for electricity and magnetism so diverse they would have amazed Nicola Tesla. I encouraged this type of thinking and once entered a physics class in a contest that called for the invention of a new board game. One of the students won over a thousand dollars for the rights to his idea while another received commendation for his cleverness.

Can we teach innovation in our schools? If we create an atmosphere for it, we will find that it is present in superfluous amounts. I would dare say that we'd be inundated with ideas if we would promote that kind of thinking. Recalling the questions from an earlier chapter asking at what point a child loses interest in school and what might be the root causes for that loss; I now ask another, at what point does a student lose his or her imagination? Knowing that a person doesn't have very many original thoughts or ideas without an imagination, interest in school must be lost somewhere between being chagrined by peer pressure and placing the desire to learn on some dusty shelf. Our right brain matter is always there waiting for us to use it.

A student with an idea needs a sounding board; someone to whom he/she can communicate those ideas for such things as feasibility, for help in determining whether it has been done before and for modification in moving their ideas from intangible to tangible. Obviously, a compassionate teacher comes to mind because ideas can also become sources of embarrassment if not handled properly, especially during critical years in a child's development. The time it takes to utter one negative comment often destroys an alliance that took years to build. It is important to have knowledgeable people available who have the capability of relating the many ideas of students to the real world as well as creating a springboard for one idea leading toward another. A curt "won't work" or "been done" will not foster an imaginative mind to bring future ideas to the table. Rather, "Let's talk about this, when would be a good time for you?" both strokes the ego and encourages students for more ideas.

Innovation needs to be processed, and schools could become a likely place to teach students how an idea moves to the marketplace. Science labs come to mind as they lay so much of the groundwork for students to search and process data on their own. Certainly we all understand that ideas need to be researched and perhaps drawn or explained in detail in order to communicate their meaning and feasibility to others. Models need to be constructed in some cases. In my experience with students, innovative ideas usually went south because a natural law had been overlooked. For example, it is physically impossible to move a 3000 pound automobile at interstate speeds expecting to get 100 miles for every gallon of gasoline burned. There is simply not the energy capable of doing this in a gallon of gasoline and all claims to the contrary are nothing more than urban legends. Theoretically one could stir a bowl of soup in order to heat it, and it is true that drinking cold water would be a way to burn calories and lose weight; but practically, neither is feasible.

But the value in each of these ideas is tremendous. Rather than telling the student that his or her ideas won't work, why not do an experiment or see if the idea holds up when crunched through an equation? In some cases the teacher could show the student certain tables in handbooks that discuss such things as the heat of combustion or ionization energies. In other situations, they could consult the World Wide Web for information. Whatever the case, the study of thermodynamics gets brought into the issue to the point of explaining feasibility, and if thermodynamics seems too high-powered the teacher can say, "Let's study some of the things that are known about heat energy." And one of the beautiful qualities of experimentation is that as one question is answered, another one is asked, which of course leads to another experiment. The promotion of innovation is a tremendous "hook" for fostering communication.

In summation, innovative students' ideas lead to knowledge; that knowledge can be shared with the rest of the class and be delivered in a manner that raises that student's esteem both of self and in the eyes of his peers. That, dear readers, is delivery of quality education and it answers the query concerning whether or not innovation can be taught in schools. It speaks of enlightenment, insight and empowerment.

-3-

What then might a curriculum consist of? In setting the parameters, a school's curriculum must first and foremost be dynamic. Being dynamic means that each student needs an electronic version of the text so, if necessary, it can be updated on a daily basis as well as having the capability of accessing corollary information. I would envision student-issued laptops that would be brought to class and turned on in much the same way students are now asked to open their textbooks. Imagine having a history text that literally includes the events of yesterday or an economics book showing the current numbers of the markets. The technology for doing this is already here and being done in varying degrees. Homework, tests, reports and in-school work can be done on the students' computers and sent immediately to the teacher's grade book for electronic grading. The same can be checked for plagiarism, as well as tagged if some in-class clandestine shenanigans might be going on. But the reformed school isn't going to tolerate the cheating problems that are found in today's public schools where over 70% of the students report they take part in cheating. Cheaters wouldn't be in a school that is a privilege to attend.

Student competition could also be eliminated because the competition would be within. Each student would be his or her own competition. In a school that is challenging, the criteria are to meet the challenges personally rather than to be rated in comparison to others. Let the standardized exams do that. A student either meets the classroom standard and passes to the next higher academic level or chooses an alternative pathway, which incidentally, is not a failure as much as it is a graduation. Failures come from being a distraction; failures come when a student fails to understand that school is serious business and if you don't understand these two things, you will not be here. Schools need to be structured so that students and parents will understand that no fork in the available pathways indicates failure of that student; different yes, but not a failure anymore than someone with an interest and love for the outdoors is better or worse than someone who likes to work with numbers. We need to throw these paradigms away.

Recently, I read that one school-age kid in five has a learning disorder—a serious problem that needs to be addressed because everyone is held to the same standard when they become adults. There are no businesses or corporations, public or private who adhere to a quota system for people with learning disorders. Whether through counseling, medications or combinations of the available resources, parents need to get to the fundamental cause of each disability in order to get their child to where they are best suited for becoming contributing, productive adults. Having some experience with students with learning disorders, it seems that concern, respect and praise for work done well goes a long way. When a learning disorder makes a student incorrigibly disorderly and disruptive, that student cannot co-exist in a classroom focused on attainment. There's a distinct difference between being habitually disruptive and a true learning disorder, and some of my most pleasant students over the years had disorders that were treated and tempered.

Early home life no doubt stereotypes a lot of disorders in children and opens the proverbial can of worms that runs the gamut of human and constitutional rights. Some parents are not ever going to be responsible and accountable. Unfortunately their children reflect it. Some parents are both responsible and accountable and no matter what, their child is not. My contention is that it is not the problem of the school to have to kowtow to certain disruptive forces at the expense of everyone. If that is what we choose to do, then we should quit calling these institutions "schools," which is the situation today for many schools are not doing what they should be doing to be worthy of the name. The network of schools throughout the country is complex, but they need to get together in a synergistic manner to make this thing called education work.

Reform School

As in all plans, the foundation must be firm, so let's make sure that in every school day there is time for physical exercise. I have often said that if I were king, I'd have all my subjects line up each morning for physical fitness. Schools should be doing the same. One place in which I taught required only one year of Physical Education and that most likely came in the freshman year so the students had three years to fatten up before graduation. This sounds cruel to say it, but the cruelty really comes from a lack of concern by both the school and parents for not teaching the importance of and the benefits from taking care of oneself. In most places Health classes are mandatory, and the subject of fitness and obesity are stressed as choices but there is little or no action taken to get fit. In our society of mega-sized food portions and a global selection of cuisines available, we have become aware of some truly serious obesity problems that present a plethora of associated maladies, yet we do little in our schools to correct their onset or heed their symptoms. What kind of love is it to take your kids to a fast food restaurant to see how many artery-clogging sandwiches they can stuff into their mouths and then spend the rest of the evening in front of a cathode ray tube of one sort or another gobbling white sugar and salt treats? It seems that in teaching health issues a study of contrasts would be in order. Passing around a section of an aorta or lung from a deceased smoker compared to a similar sample from a non-smoker is actual proof; showing pictures of genitalia infected with communicable diseases might get some attention; watching a liposuction with fat oozing out of a tube would make all students sit up and take notice. Yes, maybe it is too graphic, but…

James E. Billman

At another school where I was more involved with the physical education program, there seemed to be a correlation between those students who had excuses not to dress for P.E. and those who needed to dress and participate. Who's to blame in this case if not the parent who writes or seeks out the excuse from a health (?) official? Who's to blame when federal programs want every child to have a healthy breakfast and then the school serves them sugar-laced foods? Who's to blame when a student eats junk food like a feral dog knowing no moderation?

Sports and activities need to be discussed. To start my discussion on these issues, I would think that the fine arts should have a place in public schools but that sports should become community-sponsored activities. Both the arts and athletics require motor skills, a work ethic and time, but there is a difference that comes from our discernment of the two. I've never heard someone say that they are in school only for the spring play, but I've heard lots of old jocks tell me that they only went to school for the sports. I also know and realize that the sports connection is not only the biggest thing in town, but it is the liaison between the school and the town, especially in smaller communities. Somehow there should be more between a community and its school than sports. Considering the number of non-teaching coaches there are in schools today, I think the sports programs would be just as well off to be away from the schools. Examples that come to mind are summer youth organizations, YMCA's, little- and Babe Ruth league baseball all work without a certified teacher, a principal and an athletic director. Football is expensive for a school and in many cases, it is the revenue sport that supports all the others. There are just as many schools that lose money by playing football; just ask those teams that get pounded by 35 points every week and change coaches every full moon. Basketball doesn't require a lot of money to administer but revenues for the sport rarely, I mean rarely, come out in the black. Because of local interest in sports, particularly in view of its growth in the last forty years, high school sports would do just as well as club sports that would be supervised and administered autonomously without school participation.

In speaking of sports, community sponsored sports would allow the schools to take advantage of the opportunity to develop an active intramural program in order to expand participation by more students. In my memory, I played just as hard on the school playground as I did in any varsity sport. I realize too, that sports are often a student's ticket to college, but I don't feel whether an athlete is representing a school, town or community organization will tarnish an opportunity to play at a higher level. If I can prognosticate from what I have read about colleges and universities, they are looking at major changes for their future; changes that will include re-defining the student-athletes who represent them. In most cases, talent, like water, will find its level.

I have often given students this advice: "Play baseball until you can no longer perform to expectation." That is kind of a cryptic piece of advice but it extends to all things in life, not only baseball or sports. Whatever you do; do it until you find that you can rise no higher and then continue functioning at that level for as long as you can. That is precisely what I have been describing as my vision for educational reform throughout.

If students are going to leave school with ideas, they need to have the academic preparation to differentiate ideas from pipe dreams. There won't be the kindly old teacher to mentor them in the competitive world. The trails will not be clearly marked and there will be bears in the woods and sharks in the waters.

I wouldn't change structure as much as content. In mathematics, after young children learn their tables and the basic functions, I would suggest using the numbers as the adjectives they really are. Technical mathematics does this. In my experience, some of the students who came to the community college to become technicians in electronics and electricity had never enjoyed much success in high school math courses but thrived in technical math because the numbers took on meanings. A "5" represents very little; in fact, it's abstract until it represents something like "5 Amps," "5 Volts," or "5 harp seals." Every single problem in the technical mathematics text had a defining unit behind its number whether in full, abbreviated or represented with a Greek symbol. For example, Coulombs were divided by seconds to become Amperes and the numbers gradually became secondary to the manipulation of the units. Classical physics, as taught in high school, is actually nothing more than a math course where the numbers describe entities.

I can apply the old "I'd like to have a dollar" comment to every time I have heard students, parents or teachers tell me how difficult word problems are for them. Once the methodology is taught ("communicated" in the jargon of this text) many students find them manageable, even the more complex processes like integration that requires putting two or more equations together to get a new equation. Back in the days when teachers seemed to have more time, I thoroughly enjoyed writing word problems for my physics students by trying to make them entertaining, even into a little story. With all the other stuff that now takes teachers away from the classroom effort, the same stuff that drove me to bewilderment at the end of my career, I was lucky to have a standardized test ready in time for class. (Well, not really, but you get my drift).

In the case of learning numbers and how they interact, number arrays are helpful teaching tools that help young learners uncover patterns and recognize relationships between numbers and functions. These early "aha" discoveries are helpful in later classes that call for statistical or economic analysis. Where some educators may not have the experience or expertise that includes valuable tips to help students understand, a national curriculum could provide insights enabling them to teach however they are most comfortable. This is done in a lot of the Teacher's Editions of textbooks. In other words, we are saying "Teacher, here is what you need to teach—how you teach it is up to you." (And if you want to keep your job, you'd better teach what's in the syllabus!)

-5-

With the emphasis placed so strongly on globalization, math and science already fit the mold. The Periodic Table of the Elements is in one language and everyone uses the same version—convenient for those of us who have English as our first language. The study of natural phenomenon, barring for slight atmospheric and meteorological adjustments applies everywhere that we've been. (I'm a little reticent to call them universal laws.) Atomic theory applies as a reasonable explanation for the behavior of fundamental particles the same in Tibet as in Kansas. Scatter grams or scatter plots describe where an electron "probably" is located worldwide, and Venn diagrams explain how colors of light blend everywhere. Science and math are already global.

The teaching of science also crosses disciplines better than any other course in the curriculum. Aside from local idiosyncrasies, experimental procedures and processes are pretty much the same everywhere. Although experimentation is consistent, cultural and political policies concerning work in certain areas of bioscience sometimes run afoul of some belief systems. Reports may be language specific, but the manner in which data is treated and presented conforms to a format. Reports also use specific language; a third-person technical form that speaks universally to an end without conjecture.

In having numerous students from the Eastern Rim in class over the years, I have never seen one individual that came to the United States with poor math or science skills. Matter of fact, I never had a student from the Orient that came to school with a surly, diffident attitude either, even though they were 5000 miles from home and admittedly homesick. Most, if not all, foreign exchange students I have known cannot believe the amount of distractions and interruptions that take place in U.S. classrooms.

-6-

In discussing the Language Arts, it doesn't seem as if they are arranged quite right. If, as studies have indicated, children have the early ability in life to learn another language, foreign languages should be taught at the elementary level and concluded before a student reaches the ninth grade. I also lean toward learning two languages other than the native one for what may appear a rather contradictory reason; we learn more about our own language by learning other languages. Other languages with different word endings, sentence arrangements and tonal inflections give a "back door" look at our own. Another reason for this belief is that we learn about the culture of those who speak the language, and with that comes appreciation and understanding of co-existence. I rarely have met or listened to a teacher of a foreign language who didn't spend classroom time epitomizing the people, lifestyle and vibrancy of those who spoke the language.

No, we're not going to develop elementary kids capable of reading Cervantes' *Don Quixote* in its native Spanish anymore than we'd expect them to read Milton's *Paradise Lost*. Nor do I think that one academic year is going to turn the trick, but rather three years in each of the two foreign languages will indeed provide a pretty fair understanding and will do it with a global flair. Providing the opportunity to study other languages at a time in one's life when it is easiest for them seems rather accommodating to the student. Case in point is all the kids born in the United States whose parents or grandparents speak a language other than English at home do not have a problem speaking English at school. These kids learned a second language before the age of five.

Further, if our children became fluent in another language or two, they could talk among themselves in our presence, and we wouldn't know what they were saying...or plotting. That would be payback for all the times adults spelled out words in front of them when they were too young to understand.

I suggest the same for English classes. Regardless of the program, academic or vocational, students should know usage, syntax and expression of the same by the end of the eighth grade. To continue in school, they should be able to demonstrate a proficiency to a national standard in order to graduate into high school—no exceptions. I would also include a fair sampling of global literature to supplement the first eight years not so much to get it out of the way, but to be able to put it to work in grades 9-12.

With competency in English a "given" after eighth grade, high school will no longer be the remedial over-and-over subject that so many students find boring. High school needs to quit acquiescing to the low standards and high dichotomy that exists in these classes today in order to become more dynamic. For an eye-opening experience, one only needs to simply step into a high school English class as a substitute some morning to see some really pained-in-the-butt students.

In my observations, most middle or junior high students know that they are going to be passed into high school no matter what their performance. For the life of me, I do not understand why this is true; why a student cannot or is not given a second chance or even a third chance to learn the material they must have to meet the expectations for that grade level. If a student is trying but not achieving to standards, retaining them gives them a new chance, especially if society and peers cast off the stigma of failure put on these individuals. Sports parallels life and a

Reform School

person can strike out three times in a game and still hit a game-ending home run in the ninth inning. In not requiring standards to be met at any grade, there is no progression, no true sequence to the accomplishment brought by graduation—everything is remedial.

So how do non-readers get into high school? Schools are vehemently against bullying yet are bullied themselves when they pass students who are not performing to expectation. Schools that do this are telling us that they have no expectations, hence no performance standards. Why can't grades be based on performance as they are supposed to be and not on chronological age as they have regressed to be? I have the answer in four words: They kowtow to pressure.

As mentioned more than a few times, I am expressing my knowledge of and experiences in public education throughout the text of this book. I have spent years collecting data and sorting information into a reasonable notion of why our schools are failing. These efforts have led me to seek interviews and look at a wide assortment of jobs in and around education. Here's a question interviewers often ask prospective teachers: "What would you do if a student comes into class visibly distraught over something and causing a disturbing commotion?" The obvious answer the interviewer seeks is along the lines of soothing the savage beast, (student), talking him (why "him"?) down from his trauma and comforting him so he can settle down. The answer I offer is "I'll send him to the office because he is a distraction to the rest of the class," as I watch the frowns form on the faces of the interviewers. Another variation of the same question has been, "Do you feel that you have any problems with discipline?"

James E. Billman

My answer goes something like, "No, I remove students from my class who are discipline problems." Interviewers don't seem to care for that answer, either.

It didn't happen in my class but in another room at the school where I taught; a student was sent to the office but refused to leave the room. He continued to curse and insult everything truthful and beautiful around him so the teacher took out her cell phone and called 911. The kid thought it was just a bluff on the part of the teacher and persisted in his behavior. It wasn't a bluff. About ten minutes later, a police officer came into the room, took a minimum of abuse from the student, pulled the kid out of his seat, put him on the floor face down, handcuffed him, put him in some kind of arm lock to stand him up and took him out of the room. All this took no more than 30 seconds the way the story was related to me. It happened to be in an English class.

Just as learning to hit a golf ball takes a lot of practice swings, reading takes practice, too. Some schools have instituted free reading periods where everyone, teachers and staff included, are given time to read suitable materials of choice. When it works, it's a great idea. But if the knuckle-draggers have not been eliminated, the idea doesn't work. I mentioned previously that some textbooks might have a million words in them and that number comprises more words than some students have read in their entire lifetime counting newspapers, comic books, movie credits, signs and warnings. This is not enough to make a proficient reader. I have proposed that students who can't read to grade standard at any level should be held back and given help until they can perform adequately. On the other hand, if a student *won't* read, he or she is no longer the problem of the school but of their parents who are ultimately accountable and responsible for them. And if their parents won't take the responsibility for their children's upbringing, they should be confined in a work camp just as surely as dead-beat parents can be placed in jail. That may go too far; be too strong of an opinion, but what is the price otherwise?

-7-

Social Studies encompass that giant department that contains global information often broken into subjects such as Geography, History, Government and Sociology. Further, sociology is defined as being a study of the origin, development, structure and behavior of humans. Colleges of liberal arts go a step farther and include philosophy and religion as part of sociology and call it humanities. My suggestion is to make the social studies more responsible globally by moving more toward the inclusion of humanities in high school and junior high school curriculums. The other major change I'd suggest is to take each of the subjects as now taught individually and overlap them in the manner of a Venn diagram and call the classes Social Studies I, II, III and IV according to the year. This would certainly be monumental and would take the expertise of teachers in the social studies to organize it. The magnanimity of the undertaking would be worthy of the challenge to dedicated educators. For example, where in the study of Sociology I, II, III, and IV do we include Lee's mistakes at Gettysburg or discuss the still-present issue of women's oppression throughout so much of the world? Maybe we wouldn't discuss the former and spend much more

James E. Billman

time on the latter. Can we delete any study of the ancients like the Sumerians to gain some time?

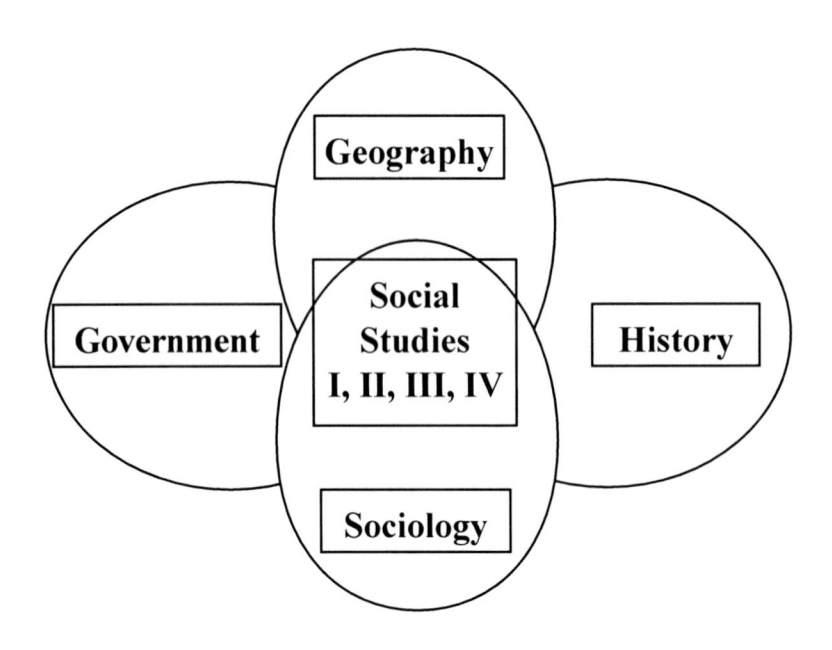

Diagram 1: The arrangement of Social Studies into a cumulative study

    I do have what seems a plausible suggestion for the social studies that allows for in-class communication, makes use of technology and combines all aspects of the social sciences at one time. From a nationally prepared, up-dated list of discussion questions or topical issues, a teacher would present something rather open-ended, but would consist of a subject that would involve more than simple conjecture. For example, take the issue concerning the merit of continuing to construct coal-fired generating plants around the world. This would be something that could be explored historically, environmentally, locally and globally. Some students would be assigned to research and report the historical aspects of using coal-fired generation. Other groups could research the alternatives and weigh the feasibilities of alternate energies. Still others would be asked to research the usage of these types of plants around the world and still others could look into the implications and humanitarian efforts to level the playing field for all people around the world. The teacher would act as the facilitator and sometimes contributor as she leads the class in their work when each of the reporting groups comes together for discussion. Students would research on their computers according to what their particular role in the lesson might be, teachers would have a guide to access and to assist them as facilitators, and the students could form their own conclusions as well as formulate solutions and ideas. New situations bring new questions and new ways in which to discuss similar issues. The I, II, III and IV would differ in depth as students progress through high school. Each discussion can differ in how it's structured for student involvement; there doesn't have to be a set format but a variety of options can be imagined to include varying summations and/or conclusions.

Incidentally, the same suggestion could apply to the natural science courses as well. (i.e., Science I, II, III, IV)

There are teachers in Social Studies who have turned their classroom into little theaters and taught from films and movies. Others rely on workbooks to supplement much of the reading and discussions from the text. I know a history teacher who starts at the present and goes back in time rather than the more traditional way. I do not know of a history teacher who covers everything from start to the present. However it is done, one school year of World History is too grandiose an undertaking to implement my

James E. Billman

notion of including the culture and history of those locations in the world we are not so familiar with. Regardless of the details of implementation, the point remains: global education is needed for global understanding; understanding that encompasses students toward awareness, toward stewardship, toward humanitarianism and toward environmentalism.

The social studies are the classes that can quite easily get students involved in the four learning styles, and the teacher that effectively does this will lead students to the aspired-to summits of understanding. Geography, history, government, sociology and philosophy allow us to positively interact and develop those ideas that will preserve, perpetuate and grow our place in the world. Schools fail their constituency when the best they can do is graduate seniors who are not willing to go forth to all corners of the globe and who are content to do no more than maintain the status quo.

-8-

On a larger scale, global economies must be understood, national strategies explained and the art of negotiation practiced in the classroom. Students should be knowledgeable concerning the events of history, but be brought to the understanding of those events from both sides of the fence. To my way of thinking, the involvement should be more than a workbook and more than a movie that places the circumstances secondary to the plot. For example, students need to understand how the effects of tariffs and trade issues extend to each of us just as well as to the more mundane things such as the wisdom of shopping at the big box stores. The social studies forum should revolve around active involvement and participation.

And at what sacrifice are we going to change the curriculum, send sports out into the community, and get everyone physically fit? I'm not sure that I've called for a longer school day or one that would change very much other than one that brings more vocational courses into specific career tracks. There could still be electives; I've often wondered where the classes are that teach etiquette, how to act formally and/or socially and perhaps how not to offend people from other cultures to name a few. It would be sad to find out that a company in United States lost a billion-dollar deal with an investor from Thailand because the American inadvertently pointed his toe at the Thai during negotiations, a blatantly offensive act.

The reformed school of my design probably would not have the structure of the ones today as much as it would be designed around the demands of the classes. In an environment where distraction is the goal for a segment of the student body, my school would remove the distractions with the message, "Come back when you can act and behave accordingly." I would expect trust because I would give trust; earn respect because I am respectful; and at all times accord a student's right to choice. If a student wants to be there they will want to do it according to the rules; if they do not want to be a part of this opportunity, they will be shown the proverbial door.

Which brings up another question: What happens to those students who are put out of school; where do they go? I have contended that they are society's problem and would expect society to respond accordingly. There will always be the private schools. Perhaps private alternative schools would also spring up. Private enterprise would focus its entrepreneurial mind to accommodate meeting the needs of these individuals. There also exists the burgeoning programs under the home schooling umbrella that could serve those needing alternative routes. Bear in mind too, that my suggestions allow for re-entry, re-routing and all sorts of shuffling around, and that I am firmly entrenched in the idea that once a no-nonsense approach to discipline is up and running in the public schools, everything else will fall into place.

Reform School

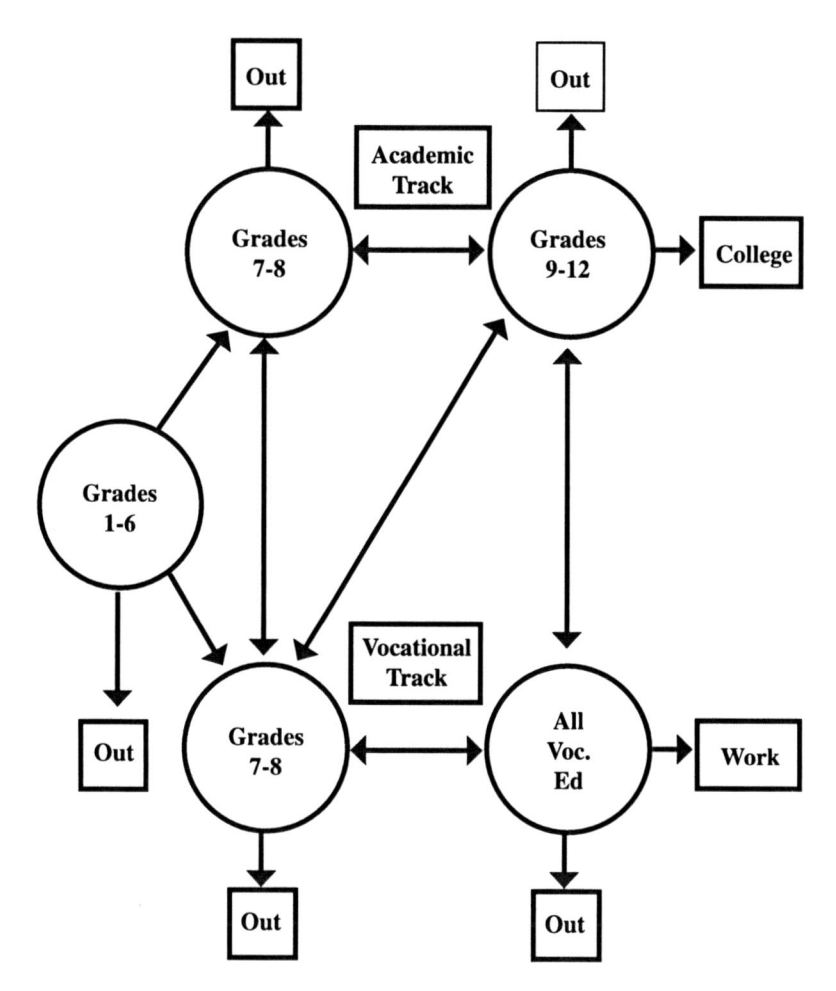

Diagram 2: Educational pathways of Reformed Public Education

In writing of innovation and ideation previously, I believe that this can be taught and that I would make it into a class unto itself in the reformed high school. A part of this class would be to provide problems that students would be asked to work on and encouraged to develop their own unique answer or solution. Again, the teacher would have a composite set of problems to chose from, some long and some short that she would offer to the class working in variously arranged manners—sometimes alone, in groups or as a class. Word problems, riddles, puzzles, architectural conundrums of history are just a few of the possibilities comprising the substance for the class. Incidentally, this would be a class for both sides of the brain. And yes, once again from a curriculum developed and offered on a national basis to all schools.

One reason I foresee the need for a national curriculum that transcends state lines is to make the school experience consistently available in order to accommodate transient students. Some schools have a yearly turn-over that involves one third of the student body. I felt so sorry for the occasional new student that I would get in the middle of a term who was given a different textbook in a similar subject but with a different arrangement. Daily class work is built sequentially around the previous day's activities of that term which makes it so hard for these new students, particularly in view of trying to "fit in" when the same bewildering thing is happening in all of their classes. This wouldn't happen if the teacher was given a nationally originated syllabus and a timeline to follow. The only difference in the classroom would be from the teacher's method of instruction that I have referred to as the individual flair. The purpose of the national syllabus would point the teacher and her class to preparing for the nationally standardized exams, if such an exam pertains to the student depending on his or her pathway.

State boundaries that impose state mandates making education on one side of a river or imaginary line different than on the other side is nuts. Do we really need 51 different Departments of Education? (Actually more exist.) I thought that

Reform School

I was a fairly successful Chemistry teacher in Iowa; the students scored well and my efforts were ratified by the administration and parents. Kentucky, on the other hand, would not certify me to teach Chemistry although I had years of experience in Iowa. Kentucky said that, based on my college hours and the fact that I could not produce a college official who would affirm my Iowa certification, I could not teach Chemistry without further course work. (I graduated in 1966. The officials of that time were long gone.) It would seem that Kentucky would benefit from my Iowa experience; my principal would have written a letter to Kentucky affirming my capability, and I could have had 50 students and 50 parents attest in my behalf for every year I taught Chemistry in Iowa. Nationalizing education and teacher certification would eliminate this kind of short-sightedness, and if I had incorrectly received accreditation from Iowa in the first place, I would have taken the course work then.

In my dismay over this experience, it has led me to think that it would not only save each and every state a lot of money to get out of educational certification but would allow teacher certification procedures to become unified. Rather than a unified, national standard, several states presently require teachers to take a course in educational law of their state for certification. Perhaps certain State's Rights regarding education needs to be re-examined for the greater good of those in school. Some states allow substitute teachers that have no degrees while others allow college graduates of any major to fill specific teaching positions. Often, these measures work very well, but much still needs to be unified to make education work everywhere.

Students also need to understand economics in view of

the global market. Not just in the sense of their community but in the sense of affectation and what options lie before them in terms of globalization. Students in this class would honestly assess and come to terms with exactly how they can impact the future. Various governments need to be explained, researched and compared in order to understand a country's mindset toward both their citizens and the rest of the world. Futurism based on trends and present conditions can be extrapolated among students as part of the class. Organizational Science should be introduced as well as the dynamics of change. Somewhere, there must be an inclusion of the human condition and the effects of war, pestilence, oppression and mass extermination. This would be another computer research class where students learn by discussing the issues offered and facilitated by the teacher on an adult level. It goes without elaboration that vibrant economies export goods because of the knowledge their graduates bring to the market.

-9-

As I might envision it, a reformed school of innovation, knowledge and ideas would allow more coming and going on the behalf of the students and would perhaps place less emphasis on being a closed society. Exceptions would exist; there is no place in any community setting for bullying, personal vendettas and racial issues. No, I wouldn't let strangers in the school; yes, I would have metal detectors and armed deputies with guard dogs because these things are necessary in our society today. But on the other hand, it is a losing battle as well as counterproductive to our basic belief system if we think we can make public gathering places fortresses of solitude. We would make our schools safer by eliminating the distractive students who are the ones responsible for most infractions.

A reformed format would arrange schools a little more differently than they are now. For example, students that are in the Building Trades tracks would have their own wing of the building, their own faculty and trainers. Then too, the level to which students aspire within a department such as the Building Trades would provide different pathways for them to choose. A finish carpenter may take longer to go through the program than a roofer, and the roofer who fabricates and cuts rafters may be in school longer than a student who does only shingling. Just think of the opportunities of choice being offered in a program like this!

Are vocational students going to take Social Studies and Natural Science courses? Yes and no, yes as the course is designed for their program, no as compared to the students going to the universities. Math is technical in the vocational programs so the mathematical expectations would involve such skills as adding fractions, reading and using a framing square, and trigonometry as it applies to framing. Efforts to change carpentry to the metric system have pretty well failed, so where a technical student would have a need to know the sum of various lengths in the English system, mathematics for the academic student might pertain more to the computer system. The systems and the pathways to graduation are based on a need to know much in the same vein as our laws are based on serving the common good.

And the biggest change that I would like to see is for

schools to be open in a different context than at present. It would be an unfair system that would not allow a student to re-train in another area. Say, for example, the roofing student mentioned above falls and sustains an injury that no longer allows him to engage in roofing. Or perhaps his body simply gets too old to conform to the shape of a roof. I say that he should be allowed to go back to school; even to the eighth grade if necessary and perhaps with a language waiver. Yes, we would have to think deeper than merely suggesting accommodations for extenuating cases. In talking to others over the years about my envisioned open school, the age issue always comes to focus. "How can thirty-year-old men go to school with sixteen-year-old girls?" they'd ask. If possible, I would not have boys and girls in the same school. And if not possible, remember that every student is honor- and duty-bound to keep school a place of serious work so when the thirty-year- old guy starts hitting on the young girls in class, he is a distraction and may place himself in even more serious trouble than getting bounced out of school. It isn't likely that a roofer who took his training and left school fifteen years ago is going to want to come back to school and enter the academic track, but we need to allow for it nevertheless.

-10-

I envision: 1) a national curriculum based on global events 2) delivered with a local flavor by teachers with 3) the capability of injecting their personal flair. I foresee a curriculum imaginative enough to include environmental issues, culture, religion and natural resources included in a discussion of economics. It is possible, even necessary to design a curriculum that teaches history from both sides and allows students to judge the effects for themselves; that promotes learning through involvement without the stigma of grades; and turns out graduates that are innovative and have substantiated ideas of their own.

There are other aspects, too. I would consider paying students who are in school. Not enough for them to buy cars and spend vacation time abroad, but enough to supplant the need for part-time jobs in order to get spending money. Imagine paying each student two thousand dollars a year to go to school from grade seven through grade twelve which presently involves, roughly speaking, about 25 million students. The total expenditure would be approximately 50 billion dollars annually, which although extremely significant, might be as good as or even better investment than bailing out institutions and businesses that have already failed. We could bring the cost down to 35 billion by just paying students in grades 9 to 12. At 50 billion, it would cost each of us about $1700 per year, but we know that's not how the government generates the bulk of its money. We could take alternate routes such as awarding graduates so much money or a set of tools commensurate with their training, or we could loan students money expecting to be paid back with interest after they graduate. There would be lots of options. Yes, I'm talking big money, but I'm also talking about our future.

Perhaps the local flavor that I speak of could rally together and support their school and invest in their futures through pledges that would go toward paying students for their efforts. Non-profit organizations and higher educational institutions presently seek people to remember them in their bequests. Although neither guaranteed nor equally distributed, such benevolence would be

James E. Billman

a big boost. Car washes and bake sales won't do it, but they could help. Maybe paying students to go to school would not work out, but it is worth being considered.

When in college, more than one of my professors spoke about privatization of education as a wave of the future. This would mean that private companies would contract the education of a school district for a period of time. Teachers, staff, books and the entire operation would come included in the "package" making use of the existing facilities. In essence every private school, from preparatory to university, already does this so why couldn't education-as-business firms work successfully for the public schools? Some schools subcontract things such as food services and custodial services so why not a cadre of professional educators? The best "why" I've heard is because local control would be relinquished.

The government's staid Job Corps does precisely this. The government provides the facility and independent, for-profit contractors agree to operate the centers to specification for a period of time. By definition, the Job Corps is a great opportunity; a no-cost educational and vocational program under the arm of the Department of Labor for men and women between the ages of 16 and 24. In addition to GED programs, on-the-job training and placement services upon graduation, participants get room and board, medical and dental services, clothing and living allowances. There are 123 of these centers scattered throughout the United States serving sixty thousand youths according to Wikipedia.

I spent a day observing the program at one center and could not believe what I saw. There were teachers extolling

Reform School

students who were sprawled in their seats to simply open their books and get started on their lessons while others were sitting and talking in conversational voices paying absolutely no attention. I watched two students pantomiming rolling and smoking a joint. This was the biggest travesty of education that I have ever seen. Granted, I was in the academic part of the program rather than the vocational end, but the students I observed were supposedly preparing themselves to enter into to the vocational program. The classes that I monitored were pure bedlam, the pay for the teachers grossly sub-standard in comparison to public schools, and the whole program operated with top-heavy diffidence. The principal was so harried that he reminded me of a pat of butter in a hot skillet. Most of the students at the facility I visited came from out-of-state and if I can believe what others said, many of these students had run afoul of the law and were given a choice between the Job Corps and jail. I can't speak for more than the one center I saw and hope this one was an isolated example on a bad day. It was hard to feel compassion or to respect the effort of the students who behaved like a bunch of thugs, but again, I saw only a small pocket over a very short time period. These programs could work by being included as part of the educational reform program I'm suggesting.

-11-

In closing, one might ask what would happen if such a wide-sweeping program of reform would come about, particularly at the onset. I would certainly expect an initial public outcry, lots of students "testing" the systems and lots of changes to go with immediate adjustments in the manner in which schools are perceived. We would need to initiate the reform with an educational program of its own, perhaps during the summer months via a number of open meetings offering the opportunity to have the system explained. We could distribute literature to the public explaining the program of educational reform through the postal system. Information could also be disseminated through the media, even the national news reports because it would be a national reform of major proportions. It is imperative that people would need to know of the changes in order to prepare for them.

Students will have to be knowledgeable of the new program before school recesses for the summer so they can register for a program that matches their aptitude and interest. It wouldn't be very sound reasoning to have a culinary program in place and no one enrolled in it. Counselors and teachers alike will have to sell the new program and relate the magnitude of the change to the students beforehand because their school lives are in for a truly major quantum shift. Interscholastic football will be gone from the schools as will mostly all the activities as they become club sports needing communal start-ups with big-time management problems. In finalizing the reform, we might find that schools would be able to circumvent the removal of sports and keep them although re-aligned to fit the new scheme; I am only making suggestions in my call for reform. Most of us wouldn't care to watch a twenty-year-old seventh grader mow over other seventh graders who are thirteen years old.

Regardless of the effort, the phone will ring in the office during that first few days when Momma calls wanting to know why her baby got kicked out of school for being a distraction.

"What do you mean a distraction; he's just being a boy!" Well Mother, you'll have to make new plans that include your son until he can follow the rules and get into a program that suits him. Mother will also need to understand that there won't be many more opportunities to re-enroll him if he continues to be a distraction. Mother should have understood this would happen and that she is both responsible and accountable for her children as a parent. She will need to undergo a paradigm shift that should have been done before now—way before now.

Here's a scenario that will increase social awareness in the public eye. Imagine that first day when 39 ninth grade boys pile into a Social Studies I classroom. (We can only imagine it because no classes should ever have more than sixteen students.) Quite a few of them are not happy with what they've been told about the new changes and consequently force the teacher to uphold the new maxims. A student acts out and is told to leave the class. Another student sounds off about the unfairness of the removal and gets the same. Still another student stands up and denounces the activity and walks out on his own accord. Then another student marches out. After ten minutes of the first class on the first day, ten students from one class are lined up in the office. Imagine too, the same thing happening in every class in the school and the line becomes 300 ex-students long.

Consider the word "ex-student" and explain why they are lined up outside the office when in reality they would be ushered out the front door into the cruel, cold world. My argument is this: students who don't want to be in school should not be forced against their will to be in school. Schools are not a place of repose for society's problems and public awareness can change this. For those who do want to be in school, there should be a real, functional system of equal opportunity across all lines and borders. We achieve the positive aspect of my wish by eliminating the negative.

Is there a "fix" to the problem of public education? Recent releases indicate that our students are presently holding their own with other countries, and even bringing their scores up from years prior. Is it enough then, to be mediocre? We Americans look at ourselves as world leaders; certainly we are the most privileged and can boast of the many educational opportunities that are provided us. Can we trust that the problems of today won't go away as easily as one generation gives way to the next? Can we gamble the future on that?

Our country's graduate schools aren't proportionately represented with our country's students which is another situation that can be disconcerting. Although we retain a good number of foreign graduate students, they won't be here if they foresee the same educational opportunity or better at home. The number of American-born physicians in the United States is also rather discouraging to many of us as we look into the crystal ball.

There are too many of these trends for us to ignore. We have nothing to lose that we haven't lost already; the only way to get it back is for change to occur through concerned citizens working together to get the proverbial ball rolling. It must be our effort for our children and for our future.

Epilogue

Although I do know that our schools are failing the majority of our students, I can't know what will happen in the future. It only seems reasonable to assume that the few pockets making inroads of educational progress will not be enough to pull our country through the straits we find ourselves in. Numerically, I contend that we are educating only ten percent of our students to their capabilities; and yes, some of this ten percent are products of public education. Rather, one might say *in spite* of public education. With neither accountability nor responsibility, public education aims for the middle and bores the upper half to distraction while leaving the lower half in its wake as it effectively reaches only a few. My objective has been to add my plea to the public outcry for educational reform and in doing so, making the point that public schools have it within their ability to reach ninety percent of all students. My hope is to generate a more concerted effort for imminent reform through the installation of only a few regulations. My suggestions may go too far for some and not far enough for others, but they seem personally tenable to me, in terms of my years of experience.

James E. Billman

    I am no pied piper calling for a following. Rather, I would hope to be a light among other lights who also know of the need for reform. There is something amiss in a country as great as ours, and I do not want to be a part of the past that brought about the failure of the present. In each of the chapters in this book, I have written to the end that our schools not only permeate but determine our quality of life.

    In making my case for a more global focus of education, I hope for a world populace that can come to understand each other. We cannot wake up next Monday morning and achieve global understanding, but we can plant the seed through education and actively nurture what grows. And initially, it has to be done with no guarantee. To merely graduate students that are innovative and who do have ideas will not guarantee them anything because we haven't done it yet. We don't know what we're capable of until we maximize our efforts. No soldier enters his first battle knowing how he will perform, but no soldier wants to go into battle unprepared and further, no soldier who finds himself in the battle wants to be a disgrace to his training; all good parallels to those in education.

    I also know that there aren't jobs for every student who may be the beneficiary of a reformed educational program geared for the twenty-first century. We're well into the Computer Age, perhaps into that segment of it that we could call the period of electronic miniaturization as we strive toward a goal of sending a message with a single electron. Yet we haven't progressed so far because today, just as it was three thousand years ago, we are searching for many answers with a limited number of resources. That's life. There will be a lot of jobs as we turn our attention to alternate energy and focus more concerted efforts of preservation upon our existing fossil fuels. There are today, and will be, more jobs in the area of bio-science whether as alternate fuel sources or in genetic research that includes everything from the food we eat to how long we can live productive lives. Alas, these jobs won't provide career positions for everybody, but they will open the door to a new arena of jobs that follow as offshoots that reach beyond current comprehension.

Service-type jobs, operators of implements, technicians and craftsmen will be needed, but not as they were forty years ago. I wrote that the Industrial Age has left us and gone elsewhere in the world and we didn't see it coming. There is no going back to the way it was just as there should be no complacency or holding pattern of stasis in the world of today. Students who have been prepared for this and who are capable of adding their input are the ones that will affect the future.

The local flavor I write of aims at people where they are and developing their ideas from that perspective, but with a global knowledge of impact. The students in the dried-up inner cities with no prospects in manufacturing have a different vantage point than the students on three-hundred acre farms that are too small to eke out a living. At polar ends to each other they are similar in the fact that both face dire straits unless they realize that no one is going to fix their problems except themselves. They can't do it without being innovative and having ideas for where they are because running away is no solution for what is left behind.

I have expressed concern over too much stratification throughout this book and struggled mightily with writing of a

James E. Billman

national curriculum as a means to that end. Recently two Los Angeles police officers told me that there were places in the city that they simply would not take me, not even under the protection of their shield. However, the same officers assured me that these areas of the city do have schools and that one of the officers had competed against these schools on the football field. There are more annual homicides in Chicago, most of which come from inner sections of the city, than there are American fatalities in Iraq. These areas have schools and cannot be overlooked. I also saw large areas of Los Angeles that were cordoned off as if to say, "No more of the same," which seems an appropriate way to end a plea, and to start a reformation.

    I hope there will be no need to write a sequel.